Big Idea to Bestseller

Jake Kelfer

Big Idea to Bestseller
How to Write, Publish, and Launch a Nonfiction Book To Grow Your Business and Make an Impact

Jake Kelfer

Copyright © 2022 –Reflek Publishing
All Rights Reserved.

No part of this publication may be reproduced, distributed, or transmitted in any form or by any means, including photocopying, recording, or other electronic or mechanical methods, without the prior written permission of the publisher, except in the case of brief quotations embodied in critical reviews and certain other noncommercial uses permitted by copyright law.

Disclaimer: The author makes no guarantees concerning the level of success you may experience by following the advice and strategies contained in this book, and you accept the risk that results will differ for each individual. The purpose of this book is to educate, entertain, and inspire.

For more information: support@jakekelfer.com

ISBN: 978-1-7378283-1-0 (print)
ISBN: 978-1-7378283-2-7 (e-book)

To everyone who has a story to tell.

HERE'S A GIFT BEFORE YOU EVEN BEGIN!

To say thanks for getting my book, here's a bonus gift to help you take action and have more fun.

Some of the free resources in this book include:

- The $100K Book Calculator –How to Make Your First or Next $100,000 From Your Book
- A Done-For-You Nonfiction Book Template –Just Plug and Play
- 25 Book Launch Ideas to Generate Your First 100 Sales
- The Writing Time Calculator to Finishing Your Book Faster Than You Ever Thought Possible
- 17 Social Media Ideas to Grow an Engaged Audience of People Ready to Buy
- The Secret SAUCE Worksheet to Creating an Elite Lead Magnet That Will Produce 1,000s of Leads from Your Book

Get your free gifts here:

www.bigideatobestseller.com/resources

Contents

Introduction ... 1

CHAPTER 1 – Your Book Is the Ultimate Differentiator ... 5

CHAPTER 2 – Why Every Entrepreneur And Business Owner Should Write A Book ... 13

CHAPTER 3 – Limiting Beliefs Stopping You from Writing Your Game-Changing Book ... 19

CHAPTER 4 – The Benefits of Self-Publishing ... 25
    Self-Publishing vs. Traditional Publishing ... 29

CHAPTER 5 – The 5 Must-Dos Before Writing ... 32

CHAPTER 6 – How To Find and Validate Your Big Idea ... 41
    How To Find Your Big Idea ... 43
    How To Validate Your Big Idea ... 45
    Picking the Right Type of Book ... 46

CHAPTER 7 – The Avengers Process To Outline Your Book ... 50

CHAPTER 8 – The Doggy Draft ... 58
    The Doggy Draft Challenge ... 61
    What To Include in Your Book ... 63
    How To Structure Your Book ... 64
    Writing Time Breakdown ... 67
    How Long To Make Your Book ... 72

Make a Lasting Impact in Real Time ... 75

CHAPTER 9 – Selective Self-Editing 77

CHAPTER 10 – Elite Editing 83
    The Different Types of Editing 84
    How To Find the Right Editor 85

CHAPTER 11 – Choosing Your Title and Subtitle 89

CHAPTER 12 – Covers That Convert 94

CHAPTER 13 – Focused Formatting 101

CHAPTER 14 – Lead Generation 105

CHAPTER 15 – Professional Publishing 115
    How To Publish Your Book on KDP 117
    How To Select Categories 118
    How To Select Your Keywords 121
    Choosing Your ISBN for Your Book 123
    Pricing Your Book 123

CHAPTER 16 – Lucrative Launching 129
    The Bestseller Launch Strategy 133
    How To Build a Launch Team 138
    How To Get Reviews 144

CHAPTER 17 – After the Launch 148
    11 Ways To Make Money from Your Book 149

BONUS CHAPTER – How To Turn Your Book into 100+ Pieces of Content 157

The Exact Roadmap from Big Idea To Bestseller 165

Here's What To Do Next 169

Acknowledgments 171

About the Author 173

Introduction

I was speaking at a conference full of entrepreneurs and I asked the audience one question:

"Have you ever read a book that changed your life?"

Every single hand went up in the room.

I then asked, "Have you ever had a checklist that's changed your life? Have you ever gotten a business card that you kept?"

The room got incredibly quiet.

No one remembers your four-step checklist. No one remembers your business cards. But people always remember a great book!

Writing a book is more than just writing a book. It is an opportunity to create someone's favorite book. How would it feel to know that your book is the book that inspired someone to make a change for the better?

It's bigger than a book!

A book is your vehicle to feeding your family.

A book is your vehicle to your dream home.

A book is your vehicle to more confidence.

A book is your vehicle to getting on stage in front of 1,000 people.

A book is your vehicle to selling your first $10K program.

A book is your vehicle to the life you've always desired.

A book is your vehicle to impacting thousands of people worldwide.

A book is your vehicle to achieving your definition of success.

I'll say it once, and I'll say it again: It's bigger than a book!

Maybe you picked this book up because you've always had a dream to write a book. Maybe you picked this up because you know how powerful a book can be for your business. Maybe it's because you are ready to take massive action to create the life of your dreams. Whatever grabbed your attention, I am grateful you are here.

I want to make something very clear right from the get-go.

I am by no means the greatest writer in the world, and I have no plans to be. What I am, however, is someone who believes in the power of story and making an impact, and I believe that sharing a message through a book is one of the most powerful things you can do for yourself, your business, and the people you aim to serve.

This book is your roadmap to writing and launching a nonfiction book. I will show you exactly how to write a high-quality book faster than you ever thought possible.

This is for you if . . .

- You've always wanted to write a book but don't know where to begin
- You don't know what to write about but know you have a story to share
- You've wondered if anyone would actually read your book
- You think writing a book takes too long
- You don't think you're a great writer
- You don't know what the steps are to writing and launching a book
- You are coachable and committed to greatness
- You want to make an impact
- You are ready to share your experiences and expertise
- You want to make a shit-ton of money

This is not for you if . . .

- You are looking for a get-rich-quick scheme
- You are not willing to do the work
- You are not interested in helping people
- You think your shit doesn't stink
- You *hate* making money

As you read this book, I encourage you to stop after each chapter and implement what you learn. If you are writing a book and using this as a guide, make sure to execute one step at a time. Don't try to skip ahead because it will slow you down and you'll have to repeat yourself. Trust the process and you will have a book before you know it!

Your book journey begins now.

Let's gooooo!

CHAPTER 1

Your Book Is the Ultimate Differentiator

"Let's get it started." –Black Eyed Peas

What do Gary Vaynerchuk, Ed Mylett, and Brené Brown all have in common?

Besides being elite entrepreneurs and world changers, they all have a book. Shoot, they all have multiple books. Take a second to think about this.

Most thought leaders have a book.

A book is the ultimate symbol of credibility and authority.

Whether writing a book has been a dream of yours for five years, five months, or the five minutes since you picked up this book, a book is—in my opinion—the ultimate differentiator for you as an entrepreneur, thought leader, or expert.

For every phase of my entrepreneurial journey, I've written a book. And each time, a book has taken my career to the next level.

I wrote my first book, *Elevate Beyond*, at twenty-three years old. At first, it was cool for me to say I had a book. I figured it would help me stand out from all the competition in the job market. What I didn't realize was how much writing a book would change my life.

When I wanted to take my speaking career to the next level, I wrote my second book, *Elevate Your Network*. That book got me invited on a speaking tour in China before the book even released, which preceded many more epic experiences that I'll remember forever.

When the pandemic hit and live speaking events shut down, I started to double down in the online world. What did I do? I wrote *The Elevated Entrepreneur* as a way to quickly scale my network and create a hugely valuable book for entrepreneurs worldwide. Writing that book immediately boosted my credibility in the online business world and it allowed me to connect with some of the top entrepreneurs in the world such as John Lee Dumas (host of *Entrepreneurs On Fire* with over one hundred million listens), Brandin Cohen (co-founder of Liquid IV), Lori Harder (top podcaster and founder of Lite Pink), Dr. Nicole LePera (creator of @the.holistic.psychologist), and many more.

Now, as I aim to inspire and assist more people in growing their business, I'm writing this book for you.

At every phase of my journey, a book has taken me to the next level both in business and my personal life, and after having thousands of readers and speaking to tens of thousands of people, I've learned that there is no better marketing asset you can have than a book.

Among the many benefits of writing a book, here are five ways you can use your book as the ultimate differentiator to separate yourself from the competition, get your time back, and impact more lives. (Yes, I said you can actually save time by writing a book. You can put in the work one time and then use your book for years to come.)

When you follow the roadmap in this book, your book can serve as the basis for months of social content, the framework for your course, the methodology for your coaching program, the content of your keynote, and much more.

Paid Product

Let's start with a no-brainer. A book is a paid product, and once you release it, you can collect a check every single month for as long as the book is around. I still get a check every month from my book that I released in 2016.

A book gives people an entry point into your world at a very affordable rate. If you have a large community, a book is a great way to get more people into your ecosystem to start learning about you and your style. If you are just beginning, a book is a great way to take all the questions you've been asked frequently and package them into a book to build your community. When people buy your book, they get to know you, your style, and your way of teaching—all of which are super valuable when it comes to inviting the reader to take the next step.

Plus, who doesn't love a little extra cash?

Networking Tool

The one thing we all desire as human beings is to feel seen, heard, and loved. When you have a book, you can gift it or share it with people, giving them the feeling of inclusion and appreciation. It's the ultimate networking tool.

Have you ever wanted to get in touch with a dream partner but had trouble getting time on their calendar or even a response back to your email?

A book can help.

Imagine this. Let's say you want to get in touch with a dream partner who can change your business overnight, but you can't seem to get a hold of them. You've tried DMing, emailing, and even filling out the contact form on their website. You've done the work and listened to their podcast, but you still can't seem to break through and find a way in.

With a book, you can reach out to their assistant or gatekeeper and ask if you can send them a gift. Oftentimes, the assistant will give you their address to send the book. Just by having a book, you went from never getting a response to having an address of the person you want to know. Then you send a signed copy of your book and include a handwritten note to make it personalized. Guess what? This note is often what you would've sent in the first email anyway.

Once you send the book to this person, they will receive a package in the mail. Everyone loves getting packages in the mail with their name on it. It's like getting a present on Hanukkah or Christmas or your birthday.

The person opens up your book and reads your note. Then they see your book and see your name on the cover. They don't have an obligation to respond, but what do *you* do when someone sends *you* a gift? You say thank you. And due to the law of reciprocity, most people will take the time to respond to said gift. You are in!

This is one way I've been able to get in contact with high-level decision-makers, podcast hosts, event coordinators, and so many other amazing people.

Customer Experience Tool

When you start with a new client, you can create an epic onboarding experience by sending them a package with a signed copy of your book. Sometimes, you can send two— one for the new client and one for them to give to a friend. We do this for every new client that joins us in our program, Big Idea To Bestseller.

When you send them the book, include a nice handwritten note welcoming them to your program or community. This gesture is incredibly appreciated, and often you'll find the client shares this gift on social media, which is great exposure for you. I've had clients share my onboarding gifts, bringing me new followers and leads.

But here's the kicker. When someone invests their hard-earned money to work with you, they want to know it's worth it. By giving them a valuable gift right from the start, you've set the stage for that client to have an incredibly positive experience. You've shown them that you care and you are invested in the relationship as well. A small act of generosity and inclusion goes a long way. When you do this, the client will come more prepared and ready, which often leads to the client taking more action, which leads to better results.

And we all know what happens when a client gets great results: they refer you to others and keep buying your stuff. Just by sending a free book and a handwritten note, you potentially created a chain reaction for someone to buy more and refer you to others. A five-dollar signed copy can turn into thousands of dollars and some amazing relationships.

Client Acquisition Tool

Let's say you have a coaching program or you are trying to secure a new speaking gig and you are in talks with a prospective client. In this case, most people who have the power to decide have a choice.

They want to make sure they pick the right person so they can get the best results. So, what do they naturally do? They start comparing you with the other options trying to figure out who they should go with. They go through the pros and cons. They watch your videos. They check out your social media and website. They comb through your testimonials.

Most of the time, all this person is looking for is a sign or a reason why they should go with you or someone else. Your book can be that reason.

Send your prospective client a signed copy of your book in advance, and this could be a gamechanger. They will feel incredibly appreciated and start thinking to themselves that if you are already delivering value and they haven't even worked with you, then imagine how great it will be when they actually sign the deal. A book gives people a reason to choose you.

I was connecting with the attendees of a conference after my keynote speech, talking with a woman who told me she was interested in writing a book. Before we went our separate ways, I gave her a copy of my book so she could see my style. A week later, she told me that she read my book on the plane and knew I was the guy to help her with her book.

Here's one more example. If Johnny and Jimmy are both incredibly great at what they do and you like both of them, but Johnny has a book and Jimmy doesn't, who are you naturally going to think is more credible?

I've asked hundreds of people this exact question, and Johnny wins almost every single time. Combine that credibility with the gift of a free book and you've found a way to separate yourself from the competition.

Lead Generation Tool

The last differentiator, for now, is leveraging your book as a free lead generation tool. (We'll talk more about lead generation in Chapter 14.) A book is an unreal way to get thousands of leads for your business, which is critical for any business to grow.

You can gift your book to ideal prospects and dream partners.

You can include bonuses and free resources in your book to get people on your email list.

You can give away a chapter on your website.

You can create an exclusive pre-launch giveaway and build your list.

You can run paid ads to a book funnel.

A book can be used in so many ways, and the crazy thing is, everyone likes to support a book launch. Writing a book is an incredible achievement, so when you have a book, people want to support. People immediately assume you know a lot about the topic if you're willing to write an entire book on it.

All you have to do is show them how to take the next step with you.

What other marketing asset can do all of this and more?

A book is the ultimate differentiator for you and your business.

It's bigger than a book!

CHAPTER 2

Why Every Entrepreneur And Business Owner Should Write A Book

You might be reading this book wondering, *Why in the world would I want to write a book?*

Maybe you've heard it could be great, but you aren't sure how it will help your business.

You might be thinking, *What are the benefits of doing this?*

Is writing a book really the best use of my time?

I have a family. I run a business. Will a book pay off for me?

Is investing in a book the right move for my business?

After helping tons of people write their books, I've come to realize there are a few core reasons people want to write a book.

#1 –High-Ticket Clients

A book gives you amazing credibility and authority. People are looking for a reason to work with you. A book gives them this reason.

By having a book, you can use it to sign more high-ticket clients at a rate you desire and deserve.

#2 –Lead Generation

One of the biggest challenges people have in growing their businesses is lead generation. A book gives you a fantastic tool to bring in new leads.

#3 –Speaking Engagements

Many event coordinators look for experts to bring in to keynote their events. When you have a book, you are viewed as an expert on your topic. That is why we encourage people to write very specific books so they can leverage it for maximum impact and gain.

Who is a decision-maker more likely to hire for an Airbnb conference: the person with no book, the person with a general real estate book, or the person with a book on how to make your first six figures on Airbnb?

By having *the* book on the topic, people see you as the person with the solution. People want their problems solved; that's why they pick up your book in the first place.

#4 –Raise Your Rates

People come to me asking all the time how they can raise their rates. I tell them to help more people solve a specific problem. I also speak honestly and tell them to do something that's worth raising your rates for.

A book is that answer. When you have a book, people see you as the expert. When you are seen as the expert, you're expected to charge accordingly.

#5 –Start a Coaching Business

Many people come to me asking for a shortcut to building a coaching business. While I believe in hard work, I also believe a book is your fast pass to success.

I was working with a client who wanted to grow her coaching business. She was struggling separating herself from all the other mindset coaches out there. She was incredible at what she did but couldn't seem to break through. She ended up writing a book, and during the week she launched her book, she signed a four-figure client.

The book was her jumpstart because people started to see her as *the* person who could help them solve a problem.

#6 –Create Social Content

Have you ever struggled with what to post on social media?

Have you ever spent hours and hours trying to come up with content that will actually grow your business?

Here's an example of time spent by an online business owner who wants to grow their business on social media:

- 45 minutes coming up with the idea
- 30 minutes creating the post

- 30 minutes thinking of some clever caption
- 15 minutes to post across social platforms

After spending close to two hours, all they have to show for it is a post or two and a lot of frustration.

When you write a book, you can turn that book into months and months of content. Not just any content, but content that you know is specific to what your ideal client is looking for.

At the end of this book, I added a bonus chapter called "How To Turn Your Book into 100+ Pieces of Content" so you can see exactly how to do this.

#7 –Create a Course

A book is an unbelievable way to create an online course. You can use the book as your framework for the course.

You can use sections of the book for different courses. As you'll see when we get to outlining the book, your book will have all the content and framework you need to create a powerful course.

#8 –Leave a Legacy

As human beings, we love to feel like we matter. We love to feel seen, heard, and loved. That is all many of us ever want.

Dale Carnegie, author of *How To Win Friends and Influence People,* once said, "Remember that a person's name is to that person, the sweetest and most important sound in any language."[1]

We want to feel significant. We want to know that our life experiences and all the shit we went through was for a reason. We want to help people. We want to be remembered.

A book gives you all of that and more. It lasts long after you're gone.

Think about it for a second. I just quoted an author who passed away decades ago. His legacy lives on through his book.

#9 –Impact a Lot of People

Every single person I've ever spoken to who's interested in writing a book wants to help people. What better way to help people than through something that has been and will be around forever?

A book gives you the chance to share your best info, your most relevant experiences, and your knowledge in an easily digestible and affordable way that people from all over the world can have access to.

Your story was meant to be shared. Your impact was meant to be made. A book will do that!

I could go on and on, but for the sake of this book, I think

---

[1] Dale Carnegie, *How to Win Friends and Influence People* (New York City, NY: Pocket Books, 1998).

you get the point. Everyone has their own reason for writing a book, but whatever your reason is, it's worth it.

You've already lived it.

You already talk about it.

You might already make money doing it.

It's time to write your book!

CHAPTER 3

Limiting Beliefs Stopping You from Writing Your Game-Changing Book

I'm not going to pretend that writing a book is easy. It's not. But hopefully these next few pages will show you that you are not alone and that you have the power to overcome some limiting beliefs. We all experience these at one point or another, and while these beliefs may be real, I want to show you how to overcome them so you can stop waiting and start acting.

#1 –I Don't Have Time

Have you ever thought you wanted to write a book only to say you don't have time? Maybe you run a business or have a family. Or maybe you do both. Maybe you travel consistently for work or the kids have practice every day. I get it! We're all busy, and we all have limited time.

When I was writing my second book, I didn't think I had any time. I was giving talks all over the country as a motivational speaker, building up the Pro Basketball Combine, and traveling across the United States on a tour I called Elevate

America where I lived in nine-plus cities for weeks at a time trying to grow my businesses. Instead of making excuses, I set aside time to work on my book for about an hour a day. A few months later, my book was ready.

When I decided to write this book, I didn't think I was going to have the time. As I began working on it, I got super clear about when I could write and for how long. I ended up spending fifty-five minutes a day on average to complete the book. During that time, I enjoyed my travels and executed on my business.

Do you have time? You only need about an hour a day.

Real talk: If something is important to you, you'll make the time to execute. If you truly honor the commitment to yourself, then you will show up and do the work.

One of our clients told me she didn't have time. She was in the process of moving and pregnant with young kids. We created the right schedule, and because she was committed, she wrote her book.

#2 –I'm Not a Writer

Believe me when I say I hear you! When I wrote my first book, I didn't associate with the identity of a writer. To be 100% honest, I didn't say I was a writer until after my second book. I didn't like writing. I didn't go to school to be a writer. But it wasn't about that. It was about sharing a message greater than myself to help people around the world solve a problem.

If your desire for impact is greater than your dislike of writing, you will write and launch a great book!

If you don't like writing, there are other ways to complete your book. You can speak it into your phone on a walk and then use a transcription service to transcribe your book. We also have programs in Big Idea To Bestseller where we can set you up with a ghostwriter who will interview you and then write your book using your words and stories and put it in your voice.

At the end of the day, you may not love writing or think you are great at it, but if you have a desire to share a message, you've gotten a result for someone else, you've gone through a personal transformation, or you are ready to have your life changed, then it's time to get started.

#3 –Who Am I To Write This Book?

Ahh, the classic question. *Who are you to write your book?* This is one of the biggest limiting beliefs I see.

I remember when I was getting ready to release my first book. I was shitting-my-pants nervous. The doubts were real, and I kept thinking in my head, *Who am I to write this book? I am twenty-three with less than a year of work experience, and I just wrote a career development book.*

It didn't help that the haters were real. People kept telling me I shouldn't release this book because I didn't have enough experience. Who's going to listen to a twenty-three-year-old on the topic of career development?

Friends were talking behind my back saying things like "Who does Jake think he is? He's crazy for retiring from the Lakers to focus on this book and build a business."

At first it was hard to ignore. I thought maybe they were right. I mean, there were people with more experience in career development than I had life experience. Who was I to release this book?

Luckily for me, I was at my parents' home (yes, I moved back home for a year after college), and I talked to my dad who is one of my heroes. I told him I was nervous and freaking out about this book. He looked at me and shared something that I'll never forget.

He said, "I don't care if you sell five copies or five million copies. When you put this book out there, great and unexpected things will happen."

Boy, was he right. I launched that book, and it went on to be my first Amazon bestseller selling thousands of copies. It launched my speaking journey at colleges nationwide, and it even was featured in college syllabi as required reading in campuses across the country.

Who are you to write the book? You are you! And that's all that matters!

#4 –There Are Already a Million Books on My Topic

Let me say this. There *are* a lot of books that exist and probably a lot that exist on your topic. However, these books aren't yours. There is someone out there in the world waiting for your book in your voice with your stories and experience.

There is someone out there right now who's read all the books you are comparing yourself to and it hasn't resonated yet. They need you, and they need what you have to say.

It is your responsibility to share your message with the world if you know it will help someone.

Plus, who cares if there are other books out there. There isn't a book out there with your stories, your experience, and your knowledge. What you have to say is a new spin that will help people.

#5 –I Don't Have Enough To Say To Write an Entire Book

You already have a book (or two) that you can write. If you've ever felt that you don't have enough to say to write a book, you're not alone, but let me break it down for you.

Have you been creating social posts for years? Let's say your average caption is two hundred words. If you are writing a 25,000-word book, that is the same amount as writing 125 captions.

Have you ever written a blog post? Let's say your blog post is 1,500 words. If you are writing a 30,000-word book, that is the same as writing twenty blog posts.

I am not saying that writing a book is the same as social

captions or blog posts, but I am saying that writing a full book is much more doable than you might think.

A coach came to me, and we started talking about her book idea. I could tell she was so passionate about writing this book, but she was so caught up on thinking she had nothing to say. I showed her the process I'm going to share with you in the coming chapters, and she quickly found that not only did she have enough to say, but she had so much to say that she needed to cut some things out. Fast-forward a few months and she ended up launching an amazing book full of great stories and lessons.

I'll say what I said at the beginning of this. Writing a book is not easy. It can be simple, but it's not easy. Don't let your mindset be an obstacle in your way any longer.

You have the skills.

You have the experience.

You have the knowledge.

You are ready to write your book!

CHAPTER 4

The Benefits of Self-Publishing

Self-publishing is becoming more and more popular as the years go on. We're seeing people who were traditionally published start to self-publish. We're seeing self-published authors sell tons of copies. We're seeing publishing houses recruit successful self-published authors to book deals. We're even seeing the book industry shift its perspective on self-publishing.

In previous decades, the only way to be really successful with your book was to get it traditionally published. That is no longer the case. You don't need an agent or a book deal to write and launch a successful book.

The big thing you need to know is if you are going to self-publish, you need to do it professionally. The biggest reason people question self-publishing is not because of who published your book but rather the quality of the published book.

I mean, when was the last time you looked at the publisher of a book? Did that impact your reading experience? Did you even know where to look?

Most people I talk to have no idea who the book publisher is. They just know if the book looks legit or amateurish.

Throughout this book, we'll talk about what you need to professionally self-publish your book so people see you and your book as legitimate, but for now, here are some benefits of self-publishing.

Credibility

The minute you release a book, you are seen as more credible. Not just that, but when you publish a book, people trust you more. Professionally self-publishing your book shows people that you are legit.

Zero Fulfillment

When you self-publish a book, you do not have to worry about fulfillment. Thanks to Kindle Direct Publishing (KDP), Amazon's self-publishing platform, you never have to worry about printing or shipping books.

KDP is a print-on-demand service, which means books are only printed when an order is placed.

Plus, when you self-publish, you don't have to have a garage full of inventory. There is no minimum order size, which is great because you don't have to worry about ordering a bunch of copies, and you don't have to spend a lot of upfront money to get large amounts of your book printed.

Instead, you can let Amazon fulfill and ship all your orders.

All you need to do is buy copies to give away and use for marketing.

Authority as the Go-To Expert

When you write a book, people assume you are more of an expert. If you've spent hours and hours putting your knowledge into a book, then you must know more than the average person.

Think about it. Books are often an author's biggest lessons or teachings condensed into a couple hundred pages. The minute I wrote a book on networking, everyone started to ask me questions about networking. When you write a book, you are seen as the expert.

Self-publishing your book gives you the opportunity to create your legacy as soon as your book is complete and published.

Nurture Your Audience

Self-publishing a book gives you an immediate in with your audience. Since you can self-publish your book as soon as it's ready, you can start using your book right away to build your audience and deepen your connection with your existing audience. When someone gets your book, they are getting to know you. They get to see your style, your personality, and your experience. In just a few hours, they get to decide whether you are the person they want helping them solve their biggest problem.

Also, where do people read books? At their desk, on a plane, or in bed. When someone reads your book, they spend hours with you. Sometimes you are even the last thought they have before sleeping and the first name they see when they wake up and see your book sitting on their nightstand.

A book allows you to create an intimate relationship with your audience and build know, like, and trust.

It's Easier Than Ever

Self-publishing a book is easier than ever before. With Kindle Direct Publishing (KDP), you can have your book uploaded in a matter of hours. The key to this is making sure you do it professionally with a fully edited manuscript, elite cover design, and well-formatted book (as you'll learn to do in the following chapters).

It's Freaking Epic!

Publishing a book is *awesome*! It is a dream come true for a lot of people.

After working with lots of authors throughout writing and launching their first book, I can tell you that once a book is released, that author immediately has more confidence in their topic. Impostor syndrome starts to disappear and confidence starts to increase because they wrote a *freaking book*!

Once confidence begins to build, it starts a chain reaction. Confidence increases, which leads to the author speaking about their book with more conviction, which makes the listener more likely to buy in, which leads to higher conversions.

Self-publishing a book has so many benefits. It's bigger than a book!

Self-Publishing vs. Traditional Publishing

Since we just talked about some of the amazing benefits of self-publishing, I think it's only right that we chat about some of the differences between self-publishing and traditional publishing.

Here's the deal. I believe there is a time and place for traditional publishing, but I believe that the majority of entrepreneurs and experts should self-publish their book.

Timeline

When you self-publish your book, you can publish it as soon as you are ready. We have worked with people who go from big idea to bestseller in as little as four months. Depending on your goals and launch strategy, this timeline can expand or contract, but the key is that you have the power to control your timeline and publish when you are ready.

When it comes to traditional publishing, it takes much longer. After doing some research and talking with friends in the industry who have traditionally published books, the average is about eighteen to thirty-six months from idea to launch.

Having flexibility on your timeline can be a massive benefit because you can time it with a launch or have it ready for a speaking engagement.

Royalties

Royalties are the amount of money an author makes per book sold.

For authors who choose to self-publish, the royalties are much higher compared to traditional publishing.

- E-book: 35%–70%
- Paperback: 60% minus printing costs

For authors who have a book deal or who seek to work with a traditional publisher, the royalties are much lower.

- Paperback: ~8%–12%

Let's say your book is 150 pages and you charge $15.95. Based on KDP's free Printing Cost & Royalty Calculator, your printing costs will be $2.65 and your royalty will be $6.92 per book. If you sell 1,000 copies that's $6,920.

Let's say your book is $15 and you get an 8% royalty rate from a publisher. That is $1.20 per book when you traditionally publish. You have to sell 5,767 copies to make the same amount.

Control/Decisions

When you self-publish your book, you maintain full control. You get to decide what editor, formatter, and cover designer you work with. You get to decide how you want to use your book. You have the freedom to create the book however you want. It's all up to you.

When you traditionally publish, there are other voices who have a say in all of this. Sometimes, depending on your deal and the advance, certain decisions are reserved for the publishing company. For some people, this is the right move for them, and I respect that as there are some great publishers and people in the industry.

Based on this breakdown, if you are looking for speed, self-publish. If you want to make more money per book sale, self-publish. If you want to have control on decisions and your creative process, self-publish.

There are some other pros and cons to both self-publishing and traditional publishing, but unless you are a celebrity, politician, or have a massive following that you know will buy tons of copies, I recommend self-publishing.

CHAPTER 5

The 5 Must-Dos Before Writing

"Failing to prepare is preparing to fail." –John Wooden

Here's what happens with a lot of people who want to write a book. They get inspired to write a book. Naturally, they think the first step is to write. While this seems like a great and logical idea, it can be a dangerous first step. They start writing, and after a chapter or two, they get stuck. They get stuck and try to figure out what should come next, but they don't know what to include or how much to share. They wait a week hoping inspiration will strike. A week turns into a month and they haven't made any progress. After a few months of this, they get discouraged. They start to think that maybe a book isn't really for them. They try again, giving it one last chance only to decide they aren't supposed to be an author.

Here's another scenario that I've seen over and over again. An author decides to write a book. They start writing and finish their first chapter. Woohoo! Then they start to edit their first chapter. They edit and edit and edit, and after a month, they start chapter two. They start to think to themselves, *If I have twelve chapters, it's going to take me well over a year to write the rough draft.* They get discouraged and say that writing a book isn't meant for them.

Has this ever happened to you?

Well, I have some good news. By using the Big Idea To Bestseller method, you will never have to experience this again. Instead, you are going to feel more confident than ever in your ability to start and finish a book. As a matter of fact, we've seen that when people follow the pre-writing steps detailed in this chapter, their chances of completing their book increase exponentially.

Just like in sports, we need to warm up before we get to game time. If we want to perform our best, we need to do the work so that when the game starts, we are ready to go.

When I played basketball, I didn't just show up five minutes before game time and hope to play well. I stretched, visualized, took warm-up shots, and got ready. The better I prepared, the better I played. When I worked with NBA athletes, they didn't just show up. They stretched with a trainer, ate a pre-game meal, went through game film, and got mentally prepared.

You should do the same for your book.

The more you prepare, the greater chance you have of performing better or, in this case, writing an incredible book that you are proud of.

I know you have a great book inside of you, so here's where we begin. Every author I work with completes these five steps before writing their first word.

#1 –Create a Commitment

The first thing you must do before writing a book is create a commitment to yourself. When you commit to yourself, you make this book a priority. And when we decide things are a priority, we always show up.

To make this official, everyone in my program signs a commitment contract. This isn't legally binding, but rather, this is for you. This is for you to commit to yourself and show up for yourself because you deserve it. You deserve to write this book, and you deserve your message to be heard.

If you want a free commitment contract to print and sign, visit www.bigideatobestseller.com/resources.

#2 –Set Your Intentions

Once you've committed to yourself that this book is a priority, it's time to set your intentions. Your intentions are your why, your purpose, your desire for writing this book. The stronger the intention, the more likely you will push through and finish this book.

One of my clients was writing her book, and about a month in, she asked to talk to me. She said she was struggling and started to wonder if writing a book was really possible for her. English was her second language, and she was nervous that the book wouldn't be any good.

I asked her, "When you started writing this book, what was your intention?" She told me that she was writing this book so her kids would know her story. I told her that's all she needs. Remember that.

A week later, we were on a call and she was full of smiles. She told me that once she reconnected with why she was doing this, she got even more committed. She got so focused that she literally locked herself in her bathroom at four a.m. in the morning to write for a few hours before the kids woke up.

I am happy to say that not only did she create a spectacular book that she is proud of, but she is now a bestselling author.

Setting your intentions is key to this process. Here are three questions to ask yourself to get clear on your intentions:

1. What is your internal intention of writing this book?
2. What is your external intention of writing this book?
3. What is your definition of success for this book?

Internal intentions tend to focus on impact and legacy. Your internal intention might be that writing a book has been a dream of yours since you were a kid. Or maybe it's that you've gone through so much shit that you feel called to share your story to help others. Or maybe you want to leave a legacy for your kids or future kids, and a book is your way of doing that.

External intentions tend to focus more on the result you want the book to bring you. This may include becoming a bestseller, starting a speaking career, building credibility as the go-to expert in your industry, signing a new client, raising your fees, or something else.

When deciding your external intention, I challenge you to be fully honest with yourself. Sometimes we struggle answering this because we don't want to seem selfish, but that's exactly why this is so important. Express your biggest dreams because if you don't declare them and believe in them, how do you expect someone else to?

Last, we need to get clear on our definition of success for the book. Just like in life, everyone has a different definition of success. Some people want to release a book because it's a passion project. Other people want to launch a book to be a bestseller. Some people say it's a successful book the minute it's published while others define success once 1,000 copies have been put in people's hands. Get specific here and get really clear on what would make your book successful.

This is not about comparing yourself to someone else. This is about declaring what you desire and making it known.

#3 –Pick Your Book Niche

Let me ask you this . . . Do you think it's easier to stand out if you wrote a book on how to lose weight or if you wrote a book on how to lose weight after forty?

The more specific you are about who you help and what you help them with, the more likely you are to stand out.

Most people want to help as many people as they possibly can, which I love, *but* trying to help everyone or solve all the problems is the fastest way to confusion. And guess what? Confused buyers don't buy.

Would you see a general doctor or a gastroenterologist if you had a stomach issue?

Would you go to a general grocery store or a deli for the freshest meat in town?

Would you go to a general business coach or a book-writing coach if you wanted to write a book?

You see a dentist when you have a tooth problem.

You visit Taco Bell when you want delicious fast food.

You see an optometrist when you have an eye problem.

With this book, be specific!

One of my favorite things to say to people is, "Your job is not to have everyone *like* you. It's to have the right people *love* you."

When picking your book niche, focus on the KPP Process.

Knowledge –What do you know?

- What have you experienced?
- How can you help provide a specific result?
- What are you incredibly talented at?

People –Who do you want to help?

- Who can you specifically help because of your experiences/knowledge?
- What are they struggling with?
- What do they need help with?

- What is stopping them?
- What outcome do they desire?

Profitable –Can you make money?

- Is there a demand for what you're providing?
- Do people want what you have to offer?
- Will people pay for what you are creating?
- What opportunities are available to you because of this?

Writing a book is an unbelievable accomplishment, but if you really want to make an impact and grow your business, then I encourage you to get super clear on your book niche.

#4 –Add "Book Time" to Your Calendar

If it's not on the calendar, it doesn't get done. We've all been here before. We think we'll remember to do something and then four days go by and we haven't done the thing we were so confident we'd remember to do. It happens to the best of us. But, when we put this task on the calendar, we are much more likely to actually complete what needs to get completed.

That is why I created Book Time. Creative, right?

Before writing your book, creating your own version of Book Time is game-changing:

- Decide how many days per week you are going to work on your book.

- Decide how long you plan to work on your book.
- Add Book Time to your calendar on those days.

This is one way of reinforcing your commitment to yourself.

Even better, this is a great way to build the habit of showing up. By the time you start writing, you'll have the habit of Book Time, which will make writing the book easier.

Just like with any new habit, this can take some adjusting and getting used to. One author I was working with struggled to find the time for Book Time, but after a few weeks, not only did she find her groove and most productive times/days but she started to crave and look forward to Book Time.

#5 –Find an Accountability Partner

Accountability is the name of the game. When we have accountability, we get more done. I could give you a statistic, but the truth is, you already know this.

Writing a book isn't something that happens overnight. It's a process that takes time, energy, and dedication. There will be times you are on top of the world, and there will be times you question everything. Having an accountability partner will keep you on track.

The big question is, Who should you have as an accountability partner? Should you have a family member? A coach? A colleague? A friend? Social media? It depends.

My mom is one of my favorite people in the world, but she is not the person I'm asking to be my accountability partner.

While she is the greatest influence in my life and I know she could hold me accountable, I'd rather keep her as my mom and my biggest supporter.

For this book, I had two main accountability partners. I had social media because I wrote this book live and documented my progress daily to thousands of people. I also had a friend from my mastermind for weekly check-ins. Each partner served a different role but both of them pushed me to show up and execute.

If you are someone that likes to make things interesting, you can create a reward or consequence. A reward could be if you finish your tasks for the week and you check in with your partner consistently, then you treat them to dinner. A consequence could be if you don't do what you say you're going to do that week then you have to donate $100 to a charity you don't agree with or give up bagels with cream cheese and lox for a month if that's your favorite breakfast.

As we go through this process, always remember to have fun.

CHAPTER 6

How To Find and Validate Your Big Idea

It was 2015 and I had just graduated from the University of Southern California. I was about to start my very first job with the Los Angeles Lakers, and I was hyped. What I didn't know at the time was how that year would impact my life.

The 2015/16 NBA season happened to be Kobe Bryant's final NBA season, so every game was electric. People would spend their life savings and travel the world just to watch Kobe play one final time. And every single game, Kobe would do his best to give his fans a memory that would last a lifetime.

To say I was inspired would be an understatement. I was absolutely FIRED UP!

I came home one night after a Lakers win and I sat on my couch before getting ready for bed. I remember sitting there in my pj's thinking about the impact that Kobe had on the world, and I thought to myself, *If he can do it, why can't I?*

Maybe I can't change the world today and inspire millions (yet) but what if I could change one person's world?

I asked myself two questions in that moment that changed the trajectory of my entire life.

What do I know? How can I help people?

Now, I'll be honest. I didn't know much even though my young twenty-three-year-old self probably thought I did. But I did know a few things. I knew how to get a dream job, how to land big internships, how to network with executives, how to get interviews, how to build a resume, how to use social media for my career, and a lot of basics about the job market as a millennial.

I have a younger brother who's one of my best friends. He's three and a half years younger than me, and at the time he was in college. I wanted a way to share all the information I had with him and the rest of his friends. Maybe I could save them time on their job hunt so they could put more energy into studying or partying or whatever they wanted to do.

So, after toying with this idea for a little, I met with a mentor of mine who was a professor at UCLA. I remember sitting down with him, telling him that I was writing some stuff to help college kids get internships and jobs. I figured he'd say that's great and encourage me to keep going, but that's not what happened.

He looked at me and calmly said, "You need to make this into a book. You have some great stuff here."

I looked back at him wildly confused and said, "You want me to write a book!? You want me to write a career development book at twenty-three years old?"

He looked at me and said, "Yes, I think it could help a lot of people."

Fast-forward five months and I released my very first bestselling book *Elevate Beyond*, which is a real-world guide to standing out in the job market and discovering your passion.

I want to make something very clear. You *do not* need to be the greatest in the world at what you do to write a great book. You just have to be one or two steps ahead of your ideal reader.

Your book is inside of you, waiting to be released.

Asking myself *What do I know?* and *How can I help people?* sparked what would become my very first book.

Now it's your turn to find your big idea.

How To Find Your Big Idea

A lot of people dream of writing a book but get stuck when it comes to deciding what to write about. Either they have a ton of ideas and can't decide which one to pick or they have no idea what to actually write about.

Picking the right book idea can sometimes be a major source of procrastination. People dance around the idea even though they know it's the right one because they're nervous that once they pick an idea, it becomes real.

It's really important to understand that you do not need to include *everything* you know in this book. The key is to focus on a specific topic to give your reader a specific result so they will ask for more information and eventually raise their hand to take the next step with you.

A big mistake authors make is they try to fit everything they've ever learned or experienced in their first book. Do not worry about sharing every life story you have. Focus on sharing what the reader needs to know to get the result you want them to get because that is what will help you establish credibility and grow your business.

To find your big idea, you have to ask yourself big questions:

- What is your coaching program/product/service that you already offer?
- What questions are you already being asked?
- What challenges does your ideal client face the most?
- What is your method to solving your clients' problems?
- What do you geek out on?
- What do people come to you for?
- What is your expertise?
- What transformation have you already gone through?

And of course, ask yourself:

- What do you know?
- How can you help?

When you ask yourself these questions, you will start to get a bunch of ideas.

How To Validate Your Big Idea

Once you have some ideas of what you can write about, you'll want to validate it and make sure it's the right idea for your book.

So how do you know which book idea is best to move forward with? Ask yourself these questions:

- PURPOSE: Which idea will help you achieve your intention?
    - If your intention is to grow your coaching business, pick the idea that is most related to your coaching so the reader can see exactly how you can help them.
- NICHE: Who is this book for? Which idea will help them get the best result?
    - If your main goal is to help real estate agents get more listings, don't pick the book idea about helping teenagers navigate puberty.
- PASSION: Which idea are you most excited about?
- SPEED: Which idea can you complete the quickest?
- COMMITMENT: Which idea are you most likely to finish?

Spend some time answering each of these questions. If you are still deciding between several topics, make a T-chart with one topic on the left and one on the right. Then answer each of these questions and see which one is more aligned with your intentions and goals.

I have a million book ideas, so when I decided I was going

to write this book, I had to figure out which idea made the most sense. I thought about my intention, my niche, what I'm excited about, and as I did that, it became incredibly clear. As soon as I realized which idea was best, I committed to it and started building out my plan.

Now that you've come up with several ideas and validated your best one, you can move forward with confidence.

Picking the Right Type of Book

Now that you've found and validated your big idea, here are the different types of books you can choose from to best share your story and message.

Guide/How-To Book

This is the style for the majority of nonfiction books written for business growth. These types of books focus on combining personal experiences with tactical information. This book you're reading is a how-to book because my goal is to help you learn how to write and launch a bestselling nonfiction book to grow your business.

Other examples include my book *Elevate Your Network*, *$100M Offers* by Alex Hormozi, and *Atomic Habits* by James Clear.

Interview Book

Interview books are where you interview people and then share their advice throughout the book. This type of book can be hugely impactful because you get to expand your network and borrow credibility from your interviewees. The downside is this type of book takes longer and there is a lot more back-end work and approvals.

A few examples are my book *The Elevated Entrepreneur*, and *Tools of Titans* and *Tribe of Mentors* by Tim Ferriss.

Quote Book

I've never met someone who's into reading, personal development, entrepreneurship, and business who doesn't love a good quote. A quote book can be great if you want to put something together pretty quickly. These are great to use as gifts for new clients or during the holidays. They are super easy reads!

One great example of a quote book is *Stay Positive* by Jon Gordon.

Daily Book

Name something more valuable than having a prospect see your name every single day for a year. We are in the business of attention, and daily books can be really powerful because you get to spend time with your ideal client every day. A daily book is a compilation of messages that you have your reader read daily.

Book Hack: If you have 365 legit posts on a particular topic, this could serve as a great daily book.

A great example of this style is *The Daily Stoic* by Ryan Holiday.

Business Fable

Business fables are fictional stories that authors tell to teach real-world lessons. These are probably the hardest to write for most people, but they can be really great because readers get so engaged and they're really easy to remember and share. They typically require more editing due to the storyline, character development, and plot.

A few examples are *The Alchemist* by Paulo Coelho, *The Go-Giver* by Bob Burg, *Energy Bus* by Jon Gordon, and *The 5 Dysfunctions of a Team* by Patrick Lencioni.

Legacy Book

Legacy books are typically books written by people after a major acquisition or at the end of a long career.

A great example of this style is *The Ride of A Lifetime* by Bob Iger (former Disney CEO).

To decide which book type is best for you, do the following:

- Go back to your intention.
- Look at your skill set.
- Look at your time frame for completion.
- What do you want to do? I mean, it is your book after all.

Most books used for business growth and credibility are guide/how-to books. When you write a how-to book, you can combine your personal experiences with your knowledge creating a great blend of entertainment and education, which allows the reader to get to know you and learn how you teach/coach/speak.

When you choose your book type, keep this in mind. A friend of mine told me when he first started his business that he wanted to deliver so much value to his audience so they would be more likely to buy his program. Because of that, he included everything he had on the topic thinking that the more he gave, the better the program would be.

What happened was the opposite.

While his intentions were great, his clients were overwhelmed. There was too much information, and his program suffered. He saw what was happening and completely redid his program. He took everything out except what was necessary for his clients to get results. Immediately people started getting huge results and his business took off.

The same concept applies to your book. You do not need to include everything that's ever happened to you in your life. You do need to include what's necessary for your reader to get the result they desire.

CHAPTER 7

The Avengers Process To Outline Your Book

Up to this point we've focused on getting you mentally prepared and set up to write an amazing book. Now is where the fun really begins.

I'm a sucker for most superhero movies, so when I came up with my updated process to outline a book, I thought it was only fitting to add some superhero mojo. Plus, you are a superhero for sharing your story and doing something so many people want to do but few have the courage to actually do.

There are three phases to The Avengers Process:

- Spider-Man
- Ant-Man
- Iron Man

Together these phases will help you put together an outline that will set you up to absolutely crush the writing phase.

Before you roll your eyes about outlining, understand that there are several ways to use your outline. Some people like to make their outline and it's the end-all be-all. Once their outline is done, they follow it to a tee. Other people like to use their outline as a loose guide that supports them on their writing journey.

Whichever type of outliner you are is perfectly okay. Find out what works for you and go all in.

The beauty of outlining is that it creates structure, and with structure comes freedom to create.

Phase 1: Spider-Man

"With great power comes great responsibility." —Uncle Ben

"With great skills and experience comes great responsibility to write a book." —Jake Kelfer

For the Spider-Man phase, we are throwing it back. Much like Tobey Maguire, Andrew Garfield, or Tom Holland glide through the air with their spider webs, we are going to create a web that will guide us through our book. I want you to imagine your favorite Spider-Man shooting webs out of his hand.

At the center of every web is the strongest point. That is where our main idea for the book goes. This is often your coaching program, expertise, or zone of genius.

In the case of this book, the center is my coaching program, Big Idea To Bestseller, which is all about helping people write and launch nonfiction books to grow their businesses and boost their credibility.

Once you've identified your core theme or main topic, it's

time to dig in. Set a timer for eighteen minutes and start drawing branches outward from the center of the web. With each branch, write things that are related to your main topic. Think about every single thing you can teach someone about your particular topic. Your goal here is to write as much as you possibly can until time is up. The Spider-Man phase focuses on the educational content for you book.

After time is up, look at all you've written. If you have more ideas, set the timer for eighteen more minutes and do it again. If you don't feel like it's complete, take a break for twenty-four hours and do it again.

Let's use this book as an example. Here's a teaser of a few concepts I wrote during my Spider-Man phase:

- Create intention around why
- What is the purpose of the book?
- How to launch
- How to find an editor
- How to get the cover designed
- How to outline my ideas
- How to write efficiently as a new author
- How to build a launch team
- How to format your book
- How to use paid promotions for launch

When you create your web, you will have a lot more ideas. Once your spider web is complete, then it's time to color code these ideas based on commonalities. If you don't have highlighters, you can just use shapes to differentiate and separate your ideas into groups.

For example, I would put how to launch, how to build a launch team, and how to use paid promotions for launch in the same color or draw squares around each.

At this point, you should start to see that a bunch of ideas actually go together under one bigger topic. These bigger topics eventually become chapters, and each idea that is colored will be a supporting point to expand upon.

If you already have a coaching program or offer, many of your chapters will be your modules/methodology.

If you refer to the example above, once I wrote all the ideas down, I started to organize them based on similarity. Here's how they break down. Notice that each bullet point is something I wrote down earlier.

Before Writing

- Create intention around why
- What is the purpose of the book?

Outline/Writing

- How to outline my ideas
- How to write efficiently as a new author

Book Production

- How to find an editor
- How to get the cover designed
- How to format your book

Launch

- How to launch
- How to build a launch team
- How to use paid promotions for launch

You can always go back to your spider web and add more to it. Actually, I recommend that. This is just the first idea drop we do!

Phase 2: Ant-Man

Now that you have a huge spider web containing all of your educational elements of what you teach, let's dive into the power of ants.

Let's be honest. A single ant is quite insignificant, but an ant colony can move mountains.

Just like a single ant can't do much, neither will one story or one testimonial or one quote. This phase is all about building out your entertainment and inspirational content of your book. The goal here is to create a bunch of talking points that help support the ideas from the Spider-Man phase.

The way we do that is create lists that work together like ants in a colony.

When you create your lists, try to come up with five to ten examples for each one.

- Stories/Personal Experiences –What stories and experiences from your life relate to your main idea?

- Key Problems You Solve – What are you actually helping a reader with?
- Testimonials/Success Stories – Who are some success stories that have come directly from your coaching/thought process?
- FAQs in Your Industry – What are people already asking you about that you speak on? What are the most common questions people have about the work you do?
- Social Media Topics – What do you speak on? What topics have you made posts on in the past?
- Quotes – What are some quotes that you really love?
- Inspiration/Other Examples – Are there stories you've read/heard from others that you want to incorporate?

Book Hack: As you build these lists, they can all be used for creating social media content. Stories become five-minute live videos. FAQs become reels. Quotes become graphics.

Once you create your lists, you can move on to the final phase where we put it all together.

Phase 3: Iron Man

The final phase to outlining your book is dedicated to one of my favorite superheroes, Iron Man.

When Iron Man was captured in the beginning of the first movie, he was told to build a weapon. Instead of building something that would harm society, he took all the raw materials he could find and secretly used them to build what became the very first Iron Man suit.

That is exactly what we aim to do in this phase. We are going to take the spider web of ideas (educational) and mix them with the lists (entertainment/inspirational) in order to create a basic chapter outline.

Before we dig into how to organize your chapters, I want you to know that everyone has a different style and different flow. What works for Susie might be different from what works for Tim. No matter what style you prefer, honor that because *you* are the secret sauce. You are what makes your book unique and special.

Okay, back to the tactics.

Many nonfiction books follow a similar framework. Maybe you've noticed this or maybe you haven't. Each chapter typically contains a mix of stories, lessons/messages, and a call to action (CTA).

Here's an example of a chapter flow:

- Chapter Title –Key topic from Spider-Man phase/name of module
- Quote (optional) –Lots of people like to start their chapter with a quote at the top
- Story –What story can you share that relates to your audience to build connection?
- Lesson –What do you want to teach the audience to help them?
- Message –What do you want the audience to take away?

- Call to Action (where applicable) –What should the audience do now?

As you write your book, you will find your flow and see what works best for you. There is no one way to do this.

I've seen people go story, lesson, story, message, CTA. I've seen others go statistic, story, lesson, testimonial, CTA. Not every chapter will be the same, but if you can leverage this framework, you will be able to connect with your reader and help them at the same time.

Do this for each chapter, and boom, your outline is created!

CHAPTER 8

The Doggy Draft

Congrats on making it this far in the book! If you've made it this far, it's clear that you are serious about writing a book that will change lives and skyrocket your business.

Growing up, I had two dogs throughout my childhood. My first dog's name was Trooper and she was a beautiful yellow lab. I still remember when I was a young kid, sitting on her like a pillow, and she was so calm about it. I remember watching the Denver Broncos play in the Super Bowl with my dad in the living room of our condo with Trooper by our side. She was our pillow while my six-year-old self ate chips and dip and stuffed my face with whatever Super Bowl goodies my parents got for us.

My other dog, Cooper, was much more energetic, and I loved him too. He was definitely a little bit louder and more rambunctious. Both of them, no matter how soft they were as pillows or how filled they were with energy, I loved it!

Like most dogs, they both barked and they both took a lot of poops. Throughout it all, our family cared for them so much and they provided us with so many amazing memories.

Writing your rough draft is kind of like having a dog. That's why we call it the Doggy Draft. It is going to make all types of noises, bring up all types of emotions, and it's going to be ruff. Plus, it's very likely that it will feel like you're constantly picking up a pile of shit as you go through the process.

But throughout it all, this rough draft will be the basis for creating epic memories and helping a lot of people feel loved, seen, and heard.

When you write a rough draft, there's this crazy notion that people expect it to be one and done. Unless you are some sort of genius, this is highly unlikely. I have never met anyone who writes one draft of their book that is ready for print.

Would you expect to be able to speak a new language after one tutoring session?

Would you expect to be able to make it to the NBA after playing basketball one time?

Would you expect to be incredible on camera after making one video?

Would you expect to be an incredible salesperson after one sales call?

Would you expect to know how to ride a bike after your first day of training?

Of course not. Yet, for some reason, we think that we should be able to write a perfect book on the first try.

Instead, the goal of your first draft is to get everything from your head onto paper, to turn your outline into written form. When you do that, the book takes on a life of its own and you start to see what it becomes.

Many people have an idea of what they want the book to be only to find out that when they start writing, it evolves and adapts into something even better than they imagined.

You will get better with practice, so give yourself some grace; there will be plenty of time later to improve the quality of the book.

One of our clients initially started writing his book about energetic balance with the hope of helping investment bankers find more balance in their lives. As he started the book, he realized it was so much more than just energetic balance. He realized that it was about helping these people find inner peace. It was more than just having great money and external validation; it was about being fulfilled and having inner peace so they could be truly happy in their life and their career. As he kept writing, the book evolved even further ultimately, being about finding inner peace, surrender, and owning your purpose. By writing his rough draft and doing the work, he figured out the true essence of his book.

Writing your rough draft is the next step to your dream book, but if you wait around and try to perfect it before you start, you'll never actually get started. You can't edit or publish something that doesn't exist, so it's time to roll up your sleeves and get writing.

The Doggy Draft Challenge

This is a concept I learned years ago that changed the entire way I viewed writing and productivity. It's called Parkinson's Law, and it states that work expands to fill the time available for completion, which basically means that if you give yourself a year to write your book, it will take you a year. But, if you give yourself thirty days, it will take you thirty days to write your rough draft.

The same applies to anything in your life. If you give yourself more time to do your house chores, it will take you that long. But, if you give yourself a deadline, you will get it done much quicker.

That is why I want to challenge you to write your first draft in thirty days or less. Before you freak out and say I'm crazy, know that this is 100% possible.

We've had clients write their rough draft in twenty-seven days, twenty-nine days, thirty-four days just to share a few.

Do some people take longer? Yes, of course. But by taking on the doggy draft challenge, it puts you in a completely new mindset, a belief that this is closer than you think.

What we've seen is that the more material you have already created (course, coaching program, blog, social content, etc.), the easier it is to formulate your draft. We've also noticed that people who took the outlining process seriously are able to execute at faster speeds than those who try to wing the whole thing.

Regardless of your starting place, writing this book is incredibly doable, and it's doable for you! You just have to honor your commitment, show up for your Book Time, and commit to consistent execution.

I heard Ed Mylett, bestselling author of *The Power Of One More*, speak at a conference, and he said that we all have a vision. If you are reading this right now, you probably have a vision of writing a book that will grow your business and share your story. He said that the problem is not that we don't have a vision, but rather we have a problem with depth perception. The difference between people who write their book and those who keep waiting is that they think a book is closer than the rest.

You see, we all have a vision, but each of us has a made-up perspective of how long writing a book will take. Maybe you don't think you can write a book that quickly because you're not a writer. Or maybe you have been told to think that it will take years of being in a log cabin to write your book. Or maybe you think only certain types of people can write a book.

Whatever you've thought up to this very moment, that's okay. It's time to change the depth perception of your vision to write this book because *it is right in front of you*. It takes thirty days of commitment to create a book you are incredibly excited about.

So I ask you right here, right now . . .

Are you ready to accept The Doggy Draft Challenge?

Let me know on Instagram @jakekelfer when you accept the challenge and write your first word. I'd love to celebrate and share your journey!

What To Include in Your Book

One of the most common questions people ask is "How much content should I give in my book? How many stories do I need to share? How much of my course do I want to give? If I give too much, will people still work with me or buy my products?"

In my opinion, after writing four books and helping tons of people write theirs, I believe that you should give the house. I believe that you should include as much as is needed to help someone get the result they want. The last thing you want to do is to make your book a pitch fest where you're constantly selling or not giving enough for them to actually get results.

I want people who read this book to get the best results possible. I am fully aware that someone might read this book and be able to write their very own bestseller and not need to hire me. My mission is to help people turn their book dreams into their reality, so I'm willing to teach a lot. At the same time, I know that people will read this book and want additional help or they will read this and refer it to their friends who need some help. It's bigger than a book!

Some people fundamentally disagree with this approach, but I love it. I want people to think that if this is my free or wildly low-ticket item, then how much better is my higher-ticket item.

There is plenty of success to go around, so help people and you will be surprised at how great things work out for you.

If you need a little more on this, think about it. People buy books all the time. Then they spend $20 on the audiobook of the same book. Then they spend $100 to get the companion course for the book. It's all the same content, but people are willing to spend more to get the content delivered in a different way.

Sure, I might miss out on some business by giving so much in this book, but that fires me up! I know there is plenty to go around and that we can all win. As one of my coaches Chris Harder says, "When good people make good money, they can do great things."

How To Structure Your Book

This is the final piece you need to write an incredible rough draft quicker than you ever thought possible.

When I was writing my first book, I had no clue what I was doing. When I was writing my second book, I got a little more specific. When I wrote my third book, my approach and style was clear. For this book, I knew exactly what I wanted to include and where.

When you have great structure, you have room for creativity. Structure when writing a book gives you the flexibility to connect the dots. It gives you space to include stories and teachings and share your life experiences. Structure allows you to get in the flow and find your voice quicker.

Let me make something very clear. Very few people pick up a book because they scroll Amazon and decide to support a random author. They buy a book for them. They buy a book because of the hope that it will solve a problem or help them achieve a desire.

When you write your book, always come from a place of how you can help the reader. What problem am I solving? What result does my reader desire? How can my transformation help someone begin theirs?

By structuring your book with intention and a focus on helping someone, you open the door to build real trust with the reader. Most of the time when I read a great book, I check out the author. I start following them on social media. If I really resonate, I go buy their programs.

When you structure your book in a way that makes sense to the reader in a logical format, you create huge opportunities for yourself and your business.

Your book does not have to be in chronological order, but it should be in the order of what makes sense to help the reader.

For example, I was working with an amazing woman on her book. The topic was around women in leadership and I asked her, "If you were to coach someone, what would be the order you would teach to help them get the results they want?"

By doing this, she created the flow of her book. She made her outline, and within a few weeks she was cruising through her first draft. At the end of thirty-two days, her draft was complete. The order of her book made sense, and she didn't have to wonder or worry about what to include or when to include it.

Earlier in the book, we broke down what a typical chapter could look like with the story, lesson, message, call to action (CTA) framework. Now, I want to share a general book framework that you can use as you write.

There are three main components to each book.

First is setting the stage and prepping the reader for an exciting experience. This should include the following:

- Problem –What is the main problem you are going to solve?
- Credibility –Why are you the person to solve this problem?
- Expectation –What should the reader expect in this book?

Some people will do this in the form of a single introduction. Others will break these into their own chapters. The key is to show you understand and can help your reader. When you do this right, you can build really great rapport from the very beginning.

The second part of your book is your solution chapters. These are the chapters where you teach your skills and knowledge. If you have a course or coaching program, this is where you include your modules. This is the meat and potatoes of your book, focusing on addressing problems and providing solutions and action steps.

The final part of the book is the wrap up. This is where you give a recap of the key points throughout your book and tell them what to do next. I like to wrap up the book with a final summary chapter, bringing the book together and leaving the reader with some inspiration. Sometimes this will include a final story or testimonial. Most people only remember a few things from your book. When you wrap up your book, this is your chance to really help the reader understand the key points and messages throughout your book.

After that, I recommend having a chapter or a few pages dedicated to what to do next. This is where you give the reader options on how to get the free resources you've shared in the book, how to continue learning and connect with you, or how to work with you.

When you follow this structure, you have everything you need to create an incredible book!

Download a free nonfiction book template at www.bigideatobestseller.com/resources.

Writing Time Breakdown

I'm not going to lie, I wish I had a cooler name for this section, but here we are.

When you write your book, it's important that you track your progress and have a system for doing so. You are busy running your business, raising your family, or enjoying your life, so it's important to know how to plan out your book.

The more clarity you have about structure and time frame, the easier it will be for you to focus on the writing part.

Whenever I build a business or start something from scratch, I always look to the numbers. Why? Because numbers don't lie.

If I wanted to make $100,000, here's how I'd break it down:

1. What is the price of my offer?
2. How many sales do I need to hit my $100,000 goal?
3. What is my conversion percentage?
4. How many calls do I need to reach the number of sales based on my conversion percentage?
5. How much outreach do I need to do to get that number of calls?

By breaking it down, the path becomes much clearer, and it starts to feel more attainable. The vision starts to feel closer. Then it becomes about doing the work.

We can do the same thing for our book.

If you want to finish your book in thirty days, here's what we need to figure out:

1. How many chapters do you have from your outline?
2. How many chapters do you need to complete per week to remain on pace?
3. How many days per week do you want to write?
4. How many chapters do you need to write per day to complete the book?

5. How long does it take per chapter? (You'll know this after two chapters.)
6. How much time per day do you actually need to complete your book?

I love math, so let me give you an example. If you want to skip this and just plug in your numbers, I've created a writing time calculator for you. Just visit www.bigideatobestseller.com/resources and you can get access to your own breakdown for free. Here we go.

1. Chapters (insert from outline)
   10 chapters

2. Chapters per week (divide total chapters by 4 weeks in a month)
   10 chapters ÷ 4 weeks = 2.5 chapters per week

3. Days per week writing (insert based on Book Time and how often you want to work on your book)
   5 days (2 days off for the weekend)

4. Chapters per day (divide days per week writing by how many chapters per week)
   5 days per week ÷ 2.5 chapters per week = 0.5 chapters per day

5. Time to write chapter (use 60 minutes first as a placeholder and then adjust once you've written a chapter or two)
   60 minutes per chapter

6. Average time writing per day to complete your book (multiply the time per chapter by how many chapters per day you need to complete)
60 minutes per chapter × 0.5 chapters per day = 30 minutes per writing session

Based on this example, you will finish a ten-chapter book in thirty days if you commit to writing five days a week, thirty minutes per day.

This is not an exact science as things evolve throughout the process, but it is an incredible way to let your mind know what's to come. It will give you peace of mind and something to target each and every day you write.

One super exciting thing that will happen for you as you begin to write is you will get into flow state. When this happens, your timeline becomes irrelevant because you will be in your own world absolutely crushing it. When I was writing my second book, I remember getting into flow state, and when I finally stopped writing, I had five of my twenty-five chapters completely written. That's 20 percent of my book complete in a single sitting.

While there will be times when writing is tough, give yourself the permission to enter flow state and crush it. Writing a book is a process, and there will be some good days full of motivation and some days when you don't want to write at all or you don't feel creative. Listen to yourself, but make sure to show up during Book Time to honor your commitment.

Now that we've laid out the math behind writing a book, let's talk about best writing practices.

- Do not edit as you write. You'll have time for that later.
- Focus on only one book at a time.
- Have both a Word doc and a Google doc.
- Save the document multiple times per writing session.
- Writing your book is your *only* priority until the draft is done. Do not worry about marketing or anything else at this point. Just get your book written. We'll have plenty of time to do everything else.
- Celebrate every chapter, every week, and every milestone as you write your book.
- Review your outline for ten to fifteen minutes before each writing session. Adjust accordingly.
- Talk to your reader as you are writing it.
- Rely on your coach/accountability partner to express yourself. You will have all the feels.
- Post on social media about your progress—first word on page, first chapter complete, etc.
- Keep going even when it's hard.

Do not edit as you go is one of the most important rules if you want to finish your rough draft quickly. This is the one rule people get stuck on because naturally you will want to edit and fix mistakes as they happen. Trust the process and just keep writing!

If you follow these tips, you will have a book written faster than you ever thought possible.

To help you write your first draft and help you execute even quicker and more efficiently, here are some productivity tips.

The first one is to use a time-tracking app called Toggl. Track your time and use that to adjust your writing breakdown and to keep you locked in. Review the data once a week so you can make sure you are on pace but also still executing everything else you need to do in your business.

Next is to use the Pomodoro Method to stay focused and disciplined. The Pomodoro Method is where you set a timer for twenty-five minutes and focus on one thing for the full twenty-five minutes. Turn off all notifications and distractions. Once the timer is up, you get a five-minute break. If you have sixty minutes a day to work on your book, you can do this twice.

Last, put your phone on Do Not Disturb when you are writing because one distraction can slow you down dramatically. Even worse, one distraction can cause you to lose your train of thought and disrupt your creative flow.

How Long To Make Your Book

The greatest thing about your book is it's yours. You have full control of what you include, how long it is, and the style you choose to use.

As great as this is, sometimes that creates what I call innovation procrastination. You have all the freedom in the world, which leads to indecision and inaction. I want to clear the air for you so you feel more confident than ever before you sit down and write your book.

If you've ever thought about writing a nonfiction book, you've probably looked up how long it should be. How many words should it be? How many chapters should it have? What should be in each chapter? Do they all have to be the same length? What are the benefits of making it longer versus shorter?

We've all been there. The real truth is your book can be whatever you want it to be. I know that isn't the answer you wanted to hear, but it's true. Books are different now than they used to be. In the past, they needed to follow a specific structure so they could get published in a traditional way. Now, we have the opportunity to be creative and do it our way.

So, here is what I tell people. How long should your book be? It should be as long as you need it to be to get the message across and help the reader get the result they desire. If that's 25,000 words, amazing. If that's 58,364 words, amazing. When writing a book to grow your business, the key is not how long it is but rather how quickly you can say what's needed to help someone solve a problem.

As a society, we continue to evolve. Our purchasing decisions and our attention spans have changed a lot. Most people want to read a book that is quick and to the point. They want to read a book and start taking action so they can get results. Few people want to read a book that takes a really long time to get to the point. They get bored and lose interest.

Let's say the average reading speed is about 250 words per minute. If you read for an hour, that's 15,000 words. Two hours is 30,000 words. And three hours is 45,000 words.

This is why I've come up with what I call the Airplane Rule. I encourage people to write a book that someone else can finish on an airplane ride. I was recently on a plane from LA to Orlando, and I decided to read. I finished the book in about two and a half hours, which as a reader made me feel incredibly accomplished. I immediately started to learn more about the author and dig into his stuff. I also felt really confident in my ability to start executing on what I learned in the book. In my opinion, this book was the perfect length because it gave me solid, tangible information and a sense of accomplishment while also not taking me forever.

People want shorter books that give them great results. Time is our most valuable resource, so if you can say the same thing in 30,000 words versus 45,000 words, wouldn't it make more sense to write 30,000 words?

Book Hack: When you publish your book and buy author copies (copies you buy at cost), the shorter your book is the cheaper each copy is to buy. This can save you hundreds or thousands of dollars when you start marketing your book.

Don't focus on trying to save a ton of money, but definitely focus on the shortest number of words you need to write to help someone get the result they desire.

Based on my experience, business books between 100–199 pages tend to sell the best, and business books 200–299 pages sell second best. Books under 99 pages or over 300 pages don't tend to do as well in this genre.

I hope this inspires you and gives you space to take a deep breath. Your book is ready to be written!

Make a Lasting Impact in Real Time

"No one has ever become poor by giving." –Anne Frank

There is one question that I've asked hundreds of entrepreneurs . . .

Why do you want to write a book?

And every single time they say because they want to make an impact. That's who we are as high performers, entrepreneurs, thought leaders, aspiring expanders. We do the things we do to help people we've never met create a better life. We create change. We inspire action. But most importantly, we create a ripple effect that goes far beyond a book.

So, I have a question for you . . .

Would you do something that takes one minute if you knew it would help someone share their story? Change someone's life? Create a ripple effect that's bigger than you? If so, I have a favor to ask you.

There are people all over the world who dream of writing a book, and when they do, it will change lives. By keeping their book inside and unwritten, they are potentially stopping someone from finding their new favorite book. The only way for us to help more people achieve their dream and create a ripple effect is to reach them, so here is my ask.

If you've found this book valuable so far, would you please take sixty seconds right now to leave an honest review wherever you bought the book? This costs sixty seconds of your time and could be the reason someone chooses to share their story and write their book.

All you have to do is say yes and you are participating in a movement that will help

- More people share their story
- More people believe their dream is possible
- More people transform their life

Together, we are changing the world one person at a time.

If you decide to leave a review right now, thank you. You are part of the movement, and through the rest of the book, you are going to find even more ways to have incredible success with your book, your business, and your life!

Just remember, a ripple effect can't always be seen, but it can always be felt.

Thank you for helping us. I appreciate you!

CHAPTER 9

Selective Self-Editing

When I was growing up, I loved math. I thought math was the greatest subject in school. I loved the way numbers made sense to me. I used to learn math tricks to the point where I could multiply any number by eleven and beat the calculator. I loved it so much I taught myself algebra in sixth grade!

When I was in seventh grade, I had a dream to play in the NBA, so I was training every day. I would come home from school and rush to play basketball, but before I could go out and shoot hoops on the driveway, I had to complete my homework. My parents were clear—no homework, no basketball.

I would rush to get it done and what I found was the faster I went, the more basic mistakes I made. Some days, my speed benefited me, and there were no mistakes. Other days, I made super simple mistakes that forced me to go back and do it again. All of these mistakes could have been avoided by checking my work. After doing this over and over again, I eventually learned to slow down, check my work, and make the adjustments, which ultimately gave me more time to play basketball. It was better to take a little longer and do it right than to rush and have to fix mistakes.

It was a valuable lesson because even though speed is incredible, there is massive value in reviewing your work. It's not always fun, but it can make all the difference.

This is true for writing a book. As quickly as I want to finish my rough draft, I still need to make sure I check my work. I need to review my work and do whatever I can to make it as good as possible before handing it off to a professional editor.

This is where the self-editing phase comes into play.

At this point, your rough draft is done! LET'S GOOOOOOO!

You now have a full book written, and momentum is picking up steam. The next phase in creating your life-changing, business-changing book is to self-edit it.

Before you start the self-editing phase, make sure to take at least twenty-four hours to celebrate finishing your book. You've just busted your butt to get this done, so enjoy it. Life is meant to be celebrated, and this is something worth celebrating! Plus, this gives you a chance to breathe and come back to the book with fresh eyes and excitement.

Book Hack: Share on social media that you finished your first draft! It's a great way to share your progress and include your audience while talking about your book.

Self-editing is your chance to go through the book, start to finish, and make your edits. As you do this, don't be alarmed as there will be lots of changes to make.

Truth be told, you are probably going to be running through all the emotions at this point. You've just crushed your rough draft and have a major sense of accomplishment, and now, I'm asking you to slow down and really dive into how to make your book better.

I'm not going to tell you self-editing is the most exciting phase of the book writing process, but it's absolutely critical as this phase will help you turn your rough draft into a polished draft ready for professional editing.

How To Self-Edit Your Book

There are two main types of self-editing that I recommend for people to go through: the verbal read through and chapter-by-chapter read through.

Verbal Read Through

Doing a verbal read through *first* will be incredibly helpful. To do this, read the book out loud as if you were speaking the book to one person. This often highlights areas that need improvement or that are really solid. As you read the book out loud, you'll find the gaps in logic and be able to make changes.

You'll also notice basic mistakes and edit them. If you wrote your rough draft without editing as you went, this is the time to fix all those grammar mistakes.

As you are reading the book out loud, ask yourself these questions:

- Does this make sense to the reader?
- Is this the message I want to share?
- Does the story come across clear and effective?
- Does the book flow well?
- If I was reading this, would I find it helpful/entertaining?

These questions will keep you on course and remind you why you are writing this book in the first place. This book is about helping someone solve a specific problem.

Chapter-by-Chapter Read Through

The chapter-by-chapter read through helps you stay organized and on track while also making sure everything gets done. It's like a reverse outline. You go through the final product and make sure that everything from the outline is shared and that your messaging is said the way you want it to be said.

As you go through self-editing, you will realize that the writer you were on chapter one most likely evolved over the course of the book. A lot of authors we work with use the beginning of the book to get things going. By the middle of the book, they are in full force, and by the end of the book they are cruising along. This is important because when you self-edit your book, you want to make sure your author style is portrayed evenly throughout the whole book.

You'll find that you can revise forever but don't get stuck spending hours and hours on one chapter. There will always be more that you can do, but as Dory said in *Finding Nemo*, "Just keep swimming."

To counter the desire to stay on the same chapter and keep revising, set a deadline for when you want to complete it. Setting a deadline will keep you moving. Once you finish each chapter, take a break and celebrate. This is a process, so make sure to celebrate the journey along the way!

Once you complete the verbal read through and chapter-by-chapter read through, you will likely feel one of two ways. You will be totally ready to pass it onto the editor or you will want to take one more look through. If you want to take one more look through, I recommend doing it in reverse order. Start with the last chapter and work your way to the beginning. The reason for this is because when we read something or look at something in the same order over and over, our mind starts to skip over things. When you read it back to front, you will be able to focus better and stay effective with your self-edits.

Here's what to keep in mind in the self-editing phase:

- There will be lots of edits to your book. Don't get frustrated.
- You may add/delete certain parts.
- You may rearrange stories/chapters as needed to work with the overall flow.
- Done is better than perfect.

- Stick to Book Time for consistent progress.
- Make a deadline for completion or else you will want to keep revising forever.
- Rely on your accountability partner.
- Reward yourself once you complete this phase.

Self-editing can feel overwhelming at times. The best way to overcome this is by breaking it down into mini action items. If you try to do this all at once just to finish quickly, you will be like my seventh-grade basketball-loving self, getting frustrated and missing mistakes or opportunities to improve. Focus on one thing at a time and you'll be done before you know it.

CHAPTER 10

Elite Editing

I'm so fired up for you as you read this book because I know what it's like on the other side of completion. I also realize that reading a super packed and tactical book on how to write and launch a book can sometimes be a lot, so here's a little verbal affirmation that will hype you up.

Repeat after me. "I AM A BESTSELLING PUBLISHED AUTHOR!"

But seriously, yell it out loud from wherever you are reading this.

"I AM A BESTSELLING PUBLISHED AUTHOR!"

There we go! You are creating the identity of the author you are becoming. Let's go!

It's time to talk about editing. Have you ever read a book with typos in it?

How did that make you feel as the reader? Did you start to question the author? Did you get annoyed and stop reading?

Getting your book professionally edited is one of the areas of your book that I encourage you to take very seriously and outsource to a professional. A poorly edited book negatively impacts the reader's experience and perspective of you and your business, which is not what we want, especially when using our book to create impact, income, and credibility.

For first-time authors, editing is often the first time someone else reads your work. This is often a critical point in the process for authors. Sometimes authors use this as a major source of procrastination. It's their first book and they've done all the work up to this point only to be scared shitless to let someone else read their work, and rightfully so. Up till now, they are the only person in the world who's read their writing. Now, they're expected to give it to a complete stranger to edit their work.

What if they change my voice? What if they don't like my book? What if it's not any good and I've been living in la-la land thinking I could do this?

These are all questions I've heard authors ask before they give their book to an editor, and I get it, but I also want you to know that an editor's job is not to pick on you or criticize you or tear you down. An editor's job is to help bring your book to life. They are professionals with the goal of helping authors turn their book into something beautiful.

The Different Types of Editing

When writing a nonfiction book, there are typically two types of editing that you will want to consider for your book: content editing and copy editing.

Content editing sometimes referred to as developmental editing is focused on the big picture. This type of editing focuses on the flow and sequencing. It helps with the content and what should be added/subtracted to make it a better reading experience. This type of editing is all about organization, writing structure, tone, and overall improvements. It's also great for making sure the messaging and audience are clear.

Copy editing is the nitty gritty. This is all about grammar, spelling, punctuation, and making sure everything makes sense. During this phase, your editor will give you suggestions on how to make the sentences stronger. Your editor will make sure the book is legit with no mistakes. This type of editing is key to making your book look and sound professional.

How To Find the Right Editor

Picking the right editor is a big deal. The right editor can really enhance your book and help you stand out. Investing in a professional editor is an investment absolutely worth making.

Don't hire your family or a friend who majored in English. Work with people who do this for a living.

Having a great editor is like hiring a superstar. Initially, you feel you can do it alone, but once you make that investment you wonder how you ever got by before. I remember when I was building the Pro Basketball Combine and I brought on our Director of Scouting. He was an absolute superstar. He did things that I didn't even know were possible, and he changed the entire event. Making that investment in him and giving him the freedom to do what he did best allowed the Pro Basketball Combine to reach new heights. This is what an editor will do for your book.

I recommend that you start looking for an editor and begin the process on the back half of your self-edit so by the time you finish, you have an editor lined up.

The first thing you want to do to find the right editor is to reach out to three to five editors. I recommend reaching out to multiple people to see how each person responds. You can use Fiverr, Upwork, Reedsy, or LinkedIn to find some really talented editors. When people work with us in our Big Idea To Bestseller program, they receive a list of top editors that I've already vetted and worked with, which saves them time and money.

When you reach out to each editor, make sure you articulate what you are looking for clearly. To save you some time, you can get a free script at www.bigideatobestseller.com/resources.

Once the editors start to respond, invite them to a call to make sure you are a good team. As great as someone is on paper, you want to make sure you vibe and have a connection.

Here are some questions to ask on a call with a potential editor:

- What is your process?
- What is your expected turnaround? (Mention your time frame)

- What is your availability for new projects?
- Are you willing to do a sample edit of a few pages or a chapter so I can see your style?
- Do you have a contract?
- What are your rates? (Get a quote)
- Why does my book interest you?

As the editor answers your questions, you will start to get a feel for them. There are four main things to look for when selecting an editor.

1. Good Relationship –You want an editor who is excited about you and your book. You want someone who you connect with rather than an editor who is just trying to get a new client.
2. Good Experience –Has the editor worked on books like yours before? Do they seem knowledgeable? Do you believe they can help you? Do you like the sample edits they did for you?
3. Good Vibe –This is your book and your team. You are in charge. Make sure that you have a good vibe with them. It will make the process a lot more fun.
4. Good Pricing –Everyone's budget for their book is different, so make sure their rate works with your budget. It's important to keep your budget in mind, but again, this is a worthwhile investment.

By the time you email three to five editors and speak with several on the phone, you will know exactly who you want to hire. At this point, trust your gut and decide.

Picking an editor can be nerve-racking, but just remember

they are the Shaq to your Kobe, the peanut butter to your jelly, the icing to your cake. With the right editor, your book will be that much better.

If you want the script to reach out to editors, visit www.bigideatobestseller.com/resources.

CHAPTER 11

Choosing Your Title and Subtitle

There are two types of people when it comes to picking a title. For some people, they've had the title of their book in their head from the very beginning. They've known what they want from the minute they had the idea. For others, this can take some serious time and thought.

Luckily for you, I've been both.

It was early 2016 and I was writing my first book. I was walking around the island in the kitchen of my parents' home thinking of what I could title my first book. I had no clue what I wanted to title it, and it was really starting to weigh on me. I'll never forget, but I just started yelling out random words that sounded cool to see if something would stick or feel right. After what felt like hours, I yelled the word *elevate*. Immediately, I felt a wave of calmness come over me. It was at that moment it finally clicked. *Elevate* was going to play a big role in my title. But I knew I needed more. *Elevate* was a great word, but what did that have to do with writing a book about the job market. I started to think about the mission behind the book and it came to me. Elevate Beyond. I wanted people to elevate beyond the norms, to rise above and land the job of their dreams.

Picking my first title was by far the hardest one. I wish I would have had a book like this to help me understand what makes a great title and subtitle.

With this book, the title was a no-brainer. My coaching program is called Big Idea To Bestseller, so naturally this book is titled "Big Idea To Bestseller." The goal of this book is to help you write and launch a book, but it's also for me to build credibility and use this book to grow my business.

Let's get clear on the purpose of the book's title and subtitle. When creating your title, you want to grab a potential reader's interest. Think of your title like a hook for an ad.

When creating a subtitle, you want to focus on showing the reader exactly what the book is about and how it will solve their problem or help them achieve the result they desire most.

As you start to think about your title for your book, remember these tips:

- Be obvious and to the point
- Make it memorable
- Focus on the main idea of the book
- Create intrigue
- Keep it simple and easy to understand

I've worked with people who create all different types of titles.

One client in the Big Idea To Bestseller program runs a nonprofit called Creating Young Minds, so when she wrote her first book, that was the obvious title.

Another client spent a lot of time trying to think of the perfect title. His book is all about having fun in the pursuit of success, so he titled his book "Enjoy the Grind."

Another one of our clients was combining spirituality with finance, so he titled his book "Banking on Angels."

Titles play a big role when it comes to selling your book. A great title will do wonders for the career of your book while a crappy title will definitely hold it back.

Let's discuss some great titles:

- Elevate Your Network
- Atomic Habits
- Never Split the Difference

While your title is about grabbing attention, your subtitle is about conveying the result someone will get by reading it. Remember, people buy books that they believe can help them. Most people don't buy books randomly just for the sake of buying a book. There's always a purpose!

If you can create a subtitle that is super clear and speaks to your ideal reader, then you immediately increase your chances of someone buying your book. If 2 percent more people buy your book because you have a clear subtitle, that could be the difference in hundreds or thousands of customers.

To craft a great subtitle, you'll want to explain what the book is and add some FUNK:

- Focus on wants/desires of the reader
- Understand how to make it specific
- Niche down
- Keywords

When you speak to the reader's desires in the subtitle, the reader starts to get excited. Have you ever read a subtitle and thought the book was made just for you? Almost like the author was inside your mind and speaking directly to you.

By adding specificity to your subtitle, you can speak the language of your ideal reader. This makes them feel seen and is a great way to build connection.

We've talked about the power of niching down when writing your book (Chapter 5). Your subtitle is a great chance to target a specific audience.

Last, use keywords in your subtitle. This will help people find your book when they search for a specific problem online.

When you add some FUNK, you can create a great subtitle!

Let's look at the subtitles to the books mentioned before:

- *Elevate Your Network: 25 Keys to Building Extraordinary Relationships in Life and Business*
- *Atomic Habits: An Easy & Proven Way To Build Good Habits & Break Bad Ones*
- *Never Split The Difference: Negotiating as if Your Life Depended on It*

If you notice, each of these subtitles are very clear and specific.

In *Elevate Your Network*, the subtitle expands on the title and tells the reader exactly what they can expect to learn in the book. It further explains the type of network I reference in the title and speaks to the reader's desire of wanting better relationships.

With *Atomic Habits*, the subtitle uses really strong keywords and phrases focusing on both sides of the habit spectrum. "Easy & Proven" makes you believe it's possible, which helps calm the reader who is nervous about if the book can actually help them. "Build Good Habits & Break Bad Ones" helps the reader solve a problem and achieve a result at the same time, which makes it more relatable.

For *Never Split The Difference*, the title is intriguing and the subtitle makes it incredibly obvious what the book is about. The best part about this subtitle in my opinion is that the author adds "As if Your Life Depended on It," which immediately raises the stakes and ties back into his brand of being an FBI negotiator.

As you start to select your title and subtitle, take your time and do this right. This will be one of the first things people see, so give them a reason to get excited and stick around.

I know that people want to make sure their title and subtitle are perfect, so I created a checklist for you to help select both your title and subtitle. Access it at www.bigideatobestseller.com/resources.

CHAPTER 12

Covers That Convert

Oh baby! It's time to create one of my favorite parts of a book—the cover.

There's something about getting your cover back from the designer that just feels right. Every time I've gotten my cover, there's been a rush of excitement. It's hard to explain, but when you get your cover, you'll get it too.

We say, "don't judge a book by its cover," but that's exactly what we do when it comes to buying a book. That is why having a great cover is so important. It is also why I encourage you to outsource this aspect of your book as well. Unless you are a professional book designer, my typical recommendation is to hire this out.

Creating a great cover is more than just designing an image and slapping your title/subtitle on the front. It's about creating a visual representation that takes your book to the next level.

To get a cover that converts, here are some things to consider that will help you execute at a high level.

E-book vs. Paperback Cover

You will need both e-book and paperback covers for your book. Your e-book cover will just be the front cover while your paperback cover will have a front cover, spine, and back cover. E-book covers tend to be easier to design since it's just the front cover, so it typically gets designed first. I recommend starting the cover design process during the editing phase to maximize your time.

Paperback covers are slightly more complex. The reason for this is because there are specifications you need to follow in order for Kindle Direct Publishing (KDP) to accept your cover. You have to upload the cover in a very specific way, which includes one design of the front cover, spine, and back cover. The front cover is the same as the e-book cover, but the spine and the back cover are designed after the book has been edited. The reason for this is because the spine is determined by the length of your book, so designing the rest of your paperback cover needs to be completed once your book is fully formatted.

Less Is More

In the movie *Forgetting Sarah Marshall*, there's a great quote from Paul Rudd where he says, "Do less." I want you to take that approach when designing your cover. Don't try to include everything you can think of. Don't try to make it the fanciest cover you've ever seen.

A great book cover is obvious not obscure. You want the reader to understand what the book is about, and you want it to stick out. When someone is scrolling through titles on Amazon, you want to be able to capture their attention right away and lure them in.

The Actual Design

When you design your cover, focus on having your title and subtitle incredibly visible. You can include an image, but it is not necessary. People naturally look at covers from top to bottom, so you'll want to include the title, subtitle, and your name in that order.

Your name should 100% be on the cover, but it doesn't need to be the focal point. I know you are excited and you want people to know it's your book, but remember, they are most likely not buying your book because of your name; they are buying the book because of what it can do for them. Plus, when you write a book that changes their life, they won't forget you. Better yet, they'll search you up and ask to work with you.

I hope this doesn't break your heart, but it's time for a hard truth: Don't use an image of yourself on the front cover. I know you are probably beautiful or a stud, and you think you should be on the front cover, but in my personal opinion, your photo should be on the back cover. The front cover is about the reader—not about you. Unless you are a celebrity or people know your face like Tony Robbins, I encourage you to put your ego aside and leave your beautiful smile off the front cover.

Now that you know what makes a great cover, it's time to

learn the process of getting this done and getting your book one step closer to completion.

#1 –Research Other Books in Your Niche

I'll be the first to admit that I had absolutely no idea what to do for the cover of my first book. So, I did what I thought any person would do. I went to Barnes & Noble and combed the nonfiction section for hours looking at other books in my niche for inspiration. I looked at which styles I enjoyed and which caught my attention. I took notes and used that to help guide my designer.

When you get ready for your cover, look on Amazon or in bookstores for inspiration from other covers. You'll likely start to see a common theme among books in particular niches. It is 100% okay to use other books for inspiration as long as you don't copy them.

#2 –Reach Out to One to Three Designers

Once you have some inspiration and a few books that you want to model your cover after, it's time to reach out to a few designers. A few great places to find designers include 100Covers, MiblArt, Fiverr, 99 Designs, and Upwork.

No matter your budget, you'll want to get the best bang for your buck.

When you reach out to the designer be clear about what you want. Just like with editing, I've included a script you can use to help you reach out to designers. Visit www.bigideatobestseller.com/resources to get it for free.

Your cover designer is another piece of your book team. Find someone that you believe will lift you up and elevate your book!

#3 –Commit to a Designer

After communicating with and looking at each designer's past work, decide. Most designers will have a satisfaction guarantee, so go for it!

#4 –Fill Out Questionnaire

Once you select your designer, they will likely have a questionnaire for you to fill out so they can better understand what you are looking for. If they don't send you a questionnaire, you'll want to send them any and all information you can. The more you give them, the more they have to work with.

As much as you want to say, "Here's my title and subtitle, work your magic," you need to give them guidance. Designers don't just wave a wand and poof, a magical design appears.

Whether through a questionnaire, phone call, or email, here's what you need to give them:

- General book description (1-to-2-sentence summary)
- Requests or ideas you have
    - What are some book cover elements you like from other books?

- What colors do you prefer?
- Is there a style you desire?
- Do you want them to use your branding?
* 3–5 other book covers you like that are in your niche
* Main categories your book will be in (keywords, genres, niches, etc.)

When you give your designer guidance, you give them space to create and do what they do best.

#5 –Get Sample Covers To Review

Depending on which designer you choose to work with, it will likely take seven to ten days to get the first round of designs. Once you get these, make sure to review them. I like to make sure there are two to three mockups so I have a few choices to work with.

#6 –Share with Social/Inner Circle for Feedback

Once you have your cover designs, it's time to get some feedback. Sharing on social or in your communities is a great way to include your audience, clients, and following in your book process. Feel free to share on Instagram stories and include a poll asking your audience to vote. Text your friends and see which cover they like best. Post on a variety of social platforms asking for feedback.

Even if you already know which design you want, this gets your people involved. They feel like they are part of your process and you get to market your book in a super organic way.

With that said, I have a huge piece of advice for you at this stage. Not all social media feedback is created equal. While it's great to include everyone, make sure that you weigh each person's feedback accordingly. The feedback you should take most seriously is from people who are in your target audience because they are actually going to be the buyers of your book. Once your book is launched, you'll want your book to sell to more than just your friends and family, which is why it is so important to have perspective.

As much as I love your high school friend Johnny, he is not the target reader for this book, so don't focus your energy on his opinion as much. Instead, focus on what your current clients or prospects think.

#7 –Make a Choice and Get Files from Designer

At this point, it's time to decide. Commit to your favorite design, one that pushes you a bit. Your book deserves to fly off the shelves. Your cover will help!

This process will lock in your front cover. Once your book is formatted, you will reach back out to your designer and have them finish the design since the page count and spine size are now solidified.

If you want the script to reach out to cover designers, visit www.bigideatobestseller.com/resources.

CHAPTER 13

Focused Formatting

Your book is edited. Your cover is designed. You are quickly approaching the finish line.

Formatting is the interior design of your book.

It's important to note that there are no official rules. There are just guidelines and suggestions from millions of other books. This is your book, so you can technically do whatever you want, but a book with bad formatting makes for a brutal reader experience, and we do not want that.

Most formatters you work with will format your book for both e-book and paperback. Each version of your book has a different type of file, and you'll need the correct files to publish your book.

Formatting is one of those things that you never really notice or think about (unless it's really bad) until it's time to do it for your book. This is one of the last tasks to do before publishing your book. When I first started writing books, I never really thought about all the things that went into a book until it was time for me to format my book. Then I was like, "Oh shit, I'm supposed to make all of those decisions."

To help you avoid this feeling of overwhelm and confusion, here are some things to think about ahead of time:

- Where do you want the page numbers? Top or bottom? Left side, centered, or right side?
- What size book do you want? I typically use 5.5" × 8.5".
- What size font do you want?
- What font type do you want?
- Are you going to have images or no images?
- What font size and styles do you want for titles? Subheadings?
- What do you want on your page headers? Name? Title? Chapter title?

As I ask these questions, you may realize you've never thought of some of these things. If that's the case, it's a great thing that you're reading this book. (By the way, thank you so much for reading this book and getting to this point. It means the world to me that you've chosen to spend time with me. And thank you for stepping up into your author identity and taking action on your book. Your book deserves to be created because there is someone out there right now who needs your book in your voice.)

Let's be real. Size matters . . .

Type also matters.

When you get your book formatted, you want to make sure that your font type and size feel good to your reader. Consider who your audience is when making this decision.

If you are speaking to people in their 60s or older, maybe consider a larger font size.

Here are a few font ideas for nonfiction books, per my formatting colleagues:

- Century
- Georgia
- Garamond
- Baskerville
- Palatino Linotype

Whatever font you choose, make sure it is easy to read when using features such as bold or italics.

When it comes to size, bigger isn't always better.

Size eleven or twelve tends to be a great range with eleven being one of the most common sizes. I encourage you to test out different fonts and sizes.

One great way to test out your font and font size before sending it to a formatter is to change various paragraphs and compare. Print out a page or two and see what feels good to you. What reads the best? What looks the best? What feels the best?

Much like finding an elite editor and a great cover designer, you're going to want to find a formatter who adds to your book team. Much like the Los Angeles Lakers in the '80s, we are building our version of Showtime as we put together our book team.

When you reach out to formatters, look for people who have a good vibe, good communication, and good experience. I totally get that you want to move fast through this process, but it's much faster to find the right person than to cut corners and have to redo it.

If you decide that you want to format your book yourself, you can use tools like Vellum or Atticus. I've always hired out the formatting, but I know a lot of people really enjoy these platforms.

Whichever direction you choose, the key is to have a book that is professionally formatted.

You can go to www.bigideatobestseller.com/resources to get a free script on how to reach out to your future all-star formatter.

CHAPTER 14

Lead Generation

If you plan to use your book to grow your business, then it is absolutely vital that you pay attention to this chapter.

How would you like to bring in hundreds or thousands of leads without any additional effort once your book is published?

In 2012, Facebook bought Instagram for one billion dollars. Many people thought this was crazy at the time, but as you know, it turned out to be a great investment. Why? Besides Instagram being an elite platform that people love, Instagram had customer data on millions and millions of people. When you acquire data, you acquire opportunity.

In order to grow your business, you need new leads. In order to attract and bring in new leads, you need a way to do that. That way is what we call a lead magnet.

A lead magnet is a gift or freebie you give to someone else in exchange for their email or phone number. For example, have you ever visited a website and seen a popup that asks for your contact info in exchange for a discount? The discount is the lead magnet because it draws you in. Or have you ever seen someone offer a free guide or training on Instagram in exchange for your name and email? In this example, the guide is the lead magnet. The better the lead magnet, the more people you will get interested in whatever it is you are offering. A strong lead magnet can bring in thousands of new leads.

Lead magnets are often something that you create to guide your prospect on a journey. When it comes to lead magnets in a book, your goal is to give the reader something that adds to the information in the book, helps them solve a specific problem, or guides them to the next step.

Lead magnets are a great way to give people a chance to further see your style and get to know you.

But why are lead magnets important?

Lead magnets are a way to turn your readers into leads. Once they become leads and are on your email or text list, you can nurture them, build a genuine connection, and guide them to the sale.

Here's what typically happens when people write and launch a book:

- They launch a book.
- They get a few sales on Amazon from friends, family, and colleagues.
- They wait and hope for business to roll in and for people to reach out.

Here's the elevated way to use your book to bring in hundreds of thousands of dollars:

- You launch a book.
- You use a clear marketing strategy.
- You include free tools/resources, a.k.a. lead magnets, in your book.
- You convert readers into leads who are asking for more information.
- You build relationships with those leads.
- You turn those leads into high-ticket clients and sales.

To take it one step further, using lead magnets to create quality leads is the difference between traffic you borrow versus traffic you own.

For example, you *do not* own your social media followers. You *do* own your email/text list. If Instagram or TikTok or any other social media platform gets shut down or your account gets blocked, your followers disappear overnight. Your email or text list doesn't. The key is to realize that lead magnets build your list, and your list is what drives connection and sales. They go hand in hand, so having a great lead magnet is critical to growth.

One of my friends had an Instagram account that was crushing it. He was building a following of tens of thousands of people, and one night, Instagram shut down his account. He spent weeks trying to get it back, but in the end, he had to start a new one. Lucky for him, he had been using lead magnets to draw his audience from Instagram to his email list. When he had to start a new account, he quickly rebuilt his following. Even better, his sales and booked calls remained relatively the same because he made his offers to his email list that he had been nurturing.

As you can see, having a lead magnet that builds your email list is huge because when you do this, you are able to connect with your audience and communicate with them regardless of what happens to social media platforms. This is why having a lead magnet is so important.

When you publish a book and see the sales start rolling in, you're going to get hyped! The only problem with this is Kindle Direct Publishing (KDP) collects all the customer data. You don't get any customer data from people who buy your books. The only way to get contact information for people who buy and read your book is through lead magnets. If you don't give people a way to connect with you or continue their journey with you, you are leaving hundreds of thousands of potential dollars on the table.

That is why we must include lead magnets in our book.

A great lead magnet not only collects information, it increases your back-end conversions and gives you the chance to build a deeper connection with someone interested in you and your offers.

In this book, I've shared several resources up to this point. If you've signed up for any of them, you'll receive instant access to whatever it is that you opted in for. Once you've done that, you will begin to receive valuable emails so we can get to know each other. The goal, first and foremost, is to give you more valuable content to help you bring your book to life. Second, it's for us to learn more about each other to the point where we can make an informed decision on whether or not we should work together. Only time will tell, but I sure hope we get the chance to make some magic happen together!

So, how do we create a lead magnet? And what is the best type of lead magnet to use?

Let's break it down.

To determine the best type of lead magnet for you and your book, focus on your skills, knowledge, and what the reader wants. I like to call this the Secret SAUCE.

S –Simple

Your lead magnet needs to focus on a singular problem. The result or promise of the lead magnet should be very obvious to the reader, making the decision to sign up incredibly easy. I know you want to help your reader, but do not try to make a lead magnet that solves everything. Focus on keeping it simple and on one problem.

A –Actionable

When you think of a lead magnet to include in your book, it needs to provide the reader with knowledge they can immediately implement. We want to help our reader see some quick wins.

U –Easy To Understand

Your lead magnet needs to be easy to interpret. There shouldn't be any confusion around what it is or how it will benefit the reader. Simply put, confused buyers don't buy. Confused readers don't opt in. Make it easy to understand.

C –Connection Based

When you create your lead magnet, it needs to reflect you and your desire to connect deeper with your reader. It should show your personality and expertise. The more you can make the reader feel like you understand them, the better off you'll be.

E –Easy To Complete

The final piece is making it easy to complete. We want the reader to have a sense of accomplishment. This makes them feel that you already helped get them results. They've read your book and now seen additional success from your lead magnet. They're likely going to want to keep working with you since they know you can help them and have already seen results.

Now that we understand exactly what a lead magnet is and why we need to include them in our book, it's time to figure out the right type of lead magnet for you and your book.

Here are some questions to get you started:

- What is your book about?
- What do people need to solve next?
- What do people need more information on before buying from you?

- What is something you can elaborate on from the book to further the readers' education?
- What is the result the audience is looking for? Can you create something to help get them there faster?
- What can you give them for free that will warm them up to want more?

I want you to know that a lead magnet doesn't have to be some fancy thing that takes you months to make. Often, lead magnets will be things you've already created that you can use. The big thing is to make sure it answers the questions above and has the Secret SAUCE.

There are so many different types of lead magnets, but when it comes to writing a book here are some of my favorites.

PDFs

These can include checklists, guides, to-do lists, top recommendations, scripts, or anything that you can create to further enhance the reader's experience.

For example, in this book, one of the lead magnets I've created is scripts so you can save hours on reaching out to editors, designers, and formatters. You can get them at www.bigideatobestseller.com/resources.

Video Content

Video is a great way to show your reader a different method of communication. They've read your book so a video can bring your personality to life. Some examples of this could be a ten-minute case study, a webinar, a training, a three-part video series, or even a how-to video on a topic further explaining a concept in the book.

Video content has huge perceived value, which means that people feel you are giving away something really good. Most people pay more for a video course than for a PDF, so having video content as a lead magnet can be really effective.

Templates

Templates are great for describing something in-depth or elaborating on a concept from the book but letting the reader plug in their personal information. This gives them a chance to see how what you describe actually works for them based on their situation. The customization is a great touch.

For example, you can get the $100K Book Calculator at www.bigideatobestseller.com/resources. This is an entirely free calculator that will let you see exactly how you can make your first or next $100K from your book. You plug in your pricing, offerings, and other information, and immediately, you're able to see the different ways you can make $100K.

Strategy Call

This is the most direct call to action you can use as a lead magnet. If you do a great job in your book, there will be people ready to take action. This is a small percentage of people, but we want to make sure we have something to offer for every stage of our journey. When you have a link to book a call, this gives people ready to work with you a super-quick way to get in touch and learn more about your offer and how you can help.

If you want to schedule a call with me and my team to help create a game plan for your book, visit www.bigideatobestseller.com/call.

Other examples of lead magnets in your book can be the audiobook, quizzes, challenges, summits, and more. The key with your book is to create and offer a lead magnet that is timeless. You don't want to offer something that is time sensitive because your book will be around for a long time, and you don't want to limit yourself.

By this point of the book, you know that I am all about taking action and making it happen.

Let's decide your lead magnet right now and put it all together. You can download a free worksheet at www.bigideatotbestseller.com/resources to help you create your lead magnet in five minutes!

- What is the topic you want to create a lead magnet for?
- What problem is this solving immediately?
- What is the delivery type (PDF, video, template, etc.)?
- What is the name of the lead magnet?
- What is included?
- Where does it go in the book (opening pages, Chapter 2, end of the book, etc.)?

When you create a lead magnet, I believe in giving something of real value. Don't just give someone something that doesn't help. Give them something so good that they will be dying to know what your paid content is like.

You have plenty of information to create a hugely successful lead magnet, but I want you to finish this chapter not only feeling inspired but also knowing the secret shortcut to maximizing your time.

When you create a lead magnet for your book, use one central hub to collect opt-ins. If you've opted in for any of my lead magnets so far, whether it's because you want them or just want to see how I do it, you'll notice there is one main link. When you opt in, it will direct you to a thank-you page where you can access all the resources in this book. So even though there are multiple lead magnets for you throughout this book, I only had to design one opt-in page and one thank-you page. This trick saved me so much time and energy on the back end. Once you've opted in to any of the resources in this book, you'll receive an email. That email will have not just the one you opted in for but all the resources I've offered in the book and further directions on how to access them.

I can't wait to see what lead magnets you decide to create in your book!

If you go to www.bigideatotbestseller.com/resources you can see exactly how I designed my opt-in page and my thank-you page that hosts all the lead magnets I share throughout this book.

CHAPTER 15

Professional Publishing

As the great Lizzo says, "It's about damn time!"

The time has come for you to publish your book. Once your book is published, the work you did can change the lives of people from around the world.

I was on the phone with someone recently, and they were flying through the book process. I mean, they were jamming. They were about three months in, and they just got their book back from the formatter. Up to this point, they had been as calm as you could be. But on this call, you could tell something was different. They started to speak with a little hesitation and concern. Their tone started to change. And then it happened.

They broke down and told me how scared they were to publish their book. They said they were feeling overwhelmed and anxious. They weren't sure if they could do it. They didn't want to put their book out in the world because they were worried about what people would think. They were concerned no one would buy it. They were afraid that they'd spent all this time writing this book and it wouldn't be any good.

I told them I knew exactly how they felt.

It was about a month before my first book was set to come out. My book was done, and now I was learning how to publish. Since it was my first book and I didn't have a coach, I was constantly reaching out to my good friend Mr. Google for advice on how to publish and launch my book. Luckily for me, Mr. Google was incredibly helpful with the tactics, but my mindset was still off.

What if no one reads my book?

What if my parents and brother are the only ones who buy it?

What if the book sucks?

Who am I to write a career development book at twenty-three?

Why did I think this was a good idea?

Should I just stop now and save myself the potential embarrassment?

All the limiting beliefs started to rush in as I got ready to publish my book.

It was then I realized this truth . . .

The desire for impact must be greater than the fear of judgment. It's bigger than the book!

I went back to my mission. I went back to why I wanted to write a book in the first place. I may not be the best writer in the world, but I knew this book had the content to change someone's life.

I thought back to the beginning. Even if I can't change the entire world, what if I can change one person's world? I decided in that moment that publishing this book was bigger than myself, and I moved forward. I haven't looked back since, and now it's your turn.

I hope that as you read this chapter, you will find that you're not alone. Publishing your book is a massive accomplishment, and when you do anything that pushes you, there will be some friction. This chapter will help you feel more confident and capable so you can share your gifts and book with the world!

How To Publish Your Book on KDP

Publishing your book the right way makes a huge difference in the success of your launch. For this book, we are going to focus mostly on publishing with Amazon's self-publishing platform called Kindle Direct Publishing (KDP). There are other ways to publish your book, but since Amazon is the biggest bookstore in the world, that's where we are going to focus our energy.

Once you make an account, you will publish your paperback and your e-book separately. The process to publish each of them is very similar, but there are a few differences.

There are three main sections to fill out and complete when you publish your book on KDP.

The first section is about the book's basic details. This is where you'll enter information such as title, subtitle, categories, keywords, book description, and more.

The second section is focused on the book's content. In the second section, you'll upload your manuscript and cover design and preview your book. You'll also select the size and other print options including a matte or glossy cover. I typically recommend 5.5" × 8.5" and a matte cover.

The final section is about distribution and pricing. Once you enter all this information, you'll be able to order your proof copy.

Some of these things are more confusing than others, so I'll discuss the ones most people have questions about.

How To Select Categories

In my opinion, after seeing hundreds of book launches, picking the right categories is one of the most important components of publishing your book if you hope to achieve bestseller status.

The mistake most people make is they try to pick the biggest categories because they think if they pick those categories, it will be seen by more people. Just like we discussed the power of writing this book for a specific person (Chapter 5), we want to select specific categories for that person.

The key is to pick the categories that give you the best chance of hitting #1.

Category –Business & Money

Subcategory –Business & Money -> Marketing & Sales

Niche Category –Business & Money -> Marketing & Sales -> Sales & Selling -> Real Estate

The difference between these is monumental. If you select the main category, you are competing with every book in the Business & Money category, whereas if you select the niche category, you are only competing against the books in the Real Estate category.

One of our clients was writing a book for athletes to help them have success on and off the court. She worked with a lot of athletes who played in college and the pros. Instead of selecting a bigger category like Sports & Outdoors, she focused on specific categories that were relevant to her book and audience, like the niche category of College & University, and when she launched, her book became a bestseller in multiple categories and was a #1 new release in five-plus categories, which increased her exposure even more.

Here's how to pick the right categories so you can publish your book correctly and set yourself up for a bestseller launch.

#1 –Identify Relevant Categories

- Search bestselling books on Amazon and find relevant niche categories.
- Click the sidebar on the left and click categories.
- Each time you pick a category, you will see more niche-specific categories populate beneath.
- Go as deep as you can until there are no more subcategories.
- Create a Google Sheet and write out twenty of those niche categories in Column A.

Make sure that you select categories that are relevant to your book. Don't pick a category like Professional Sports if your book is about affiliate marketing.

#2 –Check the #1 Book in Each Category

- See what the ranking is for each bestseller.
- The lower the ranking, the easier it is to pass them and become #1 during launch.
- Mark these on your Google Sheet in Column B.

To get more analytics and to speed up the process, you can invest in a tool like Publisher Rocket that shows you how many books you need to sell to hit #1 based on the categories.

#3 –Select Your Top Ten Categories Based on the Research

- Pick the ten most relevant categories that you want your book to be featured in.
- Save these categories as you will use all ten for launch.

#4 –Ask KDP To Add Your Book to Categories

- You will select two categories when you publish your book.
- Once your book is published, ask KDP to add your book to the ten categories you selected for maximum exposure.

If you want a template to make selecting your categories much easier, you can get one at www.bigideatobestseller.com/resources.

How To Select Your Keywords

When you are publishing your book, it will ask you for seven keywords. Keywords help your book get seen. The better your keywords are, the more likely your book will get shown to the right people.

What exactly are keywords and how do I pick the right ones?

Great question.

Keywords are words or phrases that your ideal reader is searching for. These are the words or phrases they type in when looking for a book or a resource to help solve their problem.

The better you know your ideal reader, the easier it will be to identify keywords.

When you select your keywords, understand this: You can use phrases even though it says to enter keywords. Knowing this secret is a big advantage for you because most people will just put one word. If you are able to put two to three words per phrase, you have the chance to increase your exposure and visibility. Another thing to consider is when you enter your keywords, they don't have to be exactly about your book. They can be the words or phrases that your ideal reader is looking for.

When figuring out which keywords to use, ask yourself these questions:

- Who is your reader?
- What are they actively searching for?

- What words would they use?
- What are the benefits people get from reading your book?
- What are the problems your book solves?

As you start to get ideas, you can test them out to see if people are searching them. All you have to do is go to Amazon and start typing the keywords or phrases in the search bar. Go letter by letter and see what auto-populates. These results are determined by search quantity as Amazon's goal is to help you find what you are looking for quickly so you stay on the platform and buy more stuff. Once you find some keywords or phrases that come up, mark them down.

Book Hack: When you write a phrase as a keyword, not only do you get a chance to have more than one word but Amazon actually counts every word in that phrase. If you used "how to write and launch a book on a budget" as a keyword, the algorithm sees . . .

- Write a book
- On a budget
- Launch a book
- Launch on a budget

Because of this, make sure to use all the space you can. Don't repeat words in your keyword selection. Use niche-specific phrases because they typically have less competition, which makes it easier to stand out.

Once you have your keywords, input them into KDP and keep moving forward with the publishing process.

Choosing Your ISBN for Your Book

Let me start by saying when I first heard "ISBN," I had absolutely no idea what it was. If that's you and you're thinking, *What the heck are these four letters and why do I need it?* let me show you.

An ISBN is a unique thirteen-digit identifier for your book. It stands for International Standard Book Number, and it is the global standard to identifying your book. ISBNs allow libraries, bookstores, and more to distinguish your book from the millions of others.

When you self-publish, you have two options for the ISBN. You can either have KDP assign you one or you can purchase one yourself from Bowker. Bowker is the go-to place to purchase ISBNs in the United States.

I highly encourage you to purchase one from Bowker because when you do, you can choose your publishing imprint, which makes your book look more professional. A publishing imprint is another way books are identified and are often the name of your company or brand.

There are several other advantages to having your own ISBN such as increased distribution and complete control over the metadata, a.k.a. the information that helps libraries and bookstores discover your book.

Pricing Your Book

Pricing your book can be an overwhelming task for a lot of first-time authors. It's like *Goldilocks and the Three Bears*. You don't want your price to be too low that you're skipping out on money. You don't want your price to be too high that people don't buy your book. You want it to be just right.

The important thing to note is you can price your book based on your biggest goals, and if you ever need to change it, you can. That is the beauty of self-publishing.

E-book Pricing

When pricing your e-book, there are really three main buckets to price your book. You can price low, medium, or high. Revolutionary terminology, I know. Before I share the three buckets, here is some critical information you need to know about pricing your e-book.

On KDP, you receive a royalty for every e-book that is sold.

The breakdown is as follows:

- Books priced $0.99–$2.98 have a 35% royalty, meaning you receive 35% of the sale.
- Books priced $2.99–$9.99 have a 70% royalty meaning you receive 70% of the sale.
- Books priced above $9.99 receive a 35% royalty.

Back to the three buckets of e-book pricing:

- Low –$0.99–$3.99
- Medium –$4.99–$6.99
- High –$7.99–9.99

Now let's look at a breakdown of books sold. From my

research and personal experience, e-books that are $0.99–$3.99 tend to sell at much higher rates than e-books priced $4.99 or higher. This is naturally because a cheaper price makes it easier for someone to make a quick purchasing decision. However, more book sales isn't always the right strategy.

What does this mean for you as the author? If you want to sell more books, price your e-book lower. If you want your book to be perceived as higher value, price your e-book higher.

You're probably wondering how to decide what to do. I've priced my books at every dollar amount for testing, and what I've found works best is . . . a mixture of pricing.

Let me explain.

During launch week and promo periods, which I'll discuss more in-depth in the next chapter, I set my e-book to $0.99. This allows me to capitalize on book sales and focus on my bestseller ranking. When your book is $0.99, sales skyrocket but royalties stay low. Personally, I am okay with this because I would rather shoot for bestseller ranking and get my book in thousands of people's hands rather than worry about a little more royalty money. I am more interested in people reading my book and hiring me than I am about a small royalty. If your goal is to live off your royalties, this may not be the right path for you.

Once I hit bestseller status, I start to make changes to the book pricing based on my long-term intentions and goals.

If you are looking to sell a shit-ton of copies, keep your book priced low. If you are looking to have your book seen as high value or you are offering it elsewhere and you want people to buy it there rather than Amazon, it might be a good idea to set the price high on KDP. If you want to have a mix of sales and perceived value, go ahead and set your price in the medium bucket.

Ultimately, this decision is yours. Focus on the bigger picture of why you are writing this book.

Paperback Pricing

Pricing your paperback is slightly easier in my opinion than pricing your e-book for a few reasons.

There is much less strategy when it comes to bestseller rankings, and there is no difference in royalties based on price. No matter what your price is, you still get the same royalty. Paperback royalties are 60% of the list price minus your printing costs. You can use the KDP Printing Cost & Royalty Calculator to see how much you earn per book sold.

Because of this, you want to determine your price based on your goals. One goal an author might have is wanting to earn a certain amount per book while another author might want to charge more per book because they want the book to appear more valuable or they want people to buy it elsewhere.

When it comes to pricing your paperback, I consider three buckets:

- Low –$11.99–$13.99
- Medium –$14.99–$16.99
- High –$17.99–$19.99

To put this in perspective, I launched my first two books *Elevate Beyond* and *Elevate Your Network* at $15.95 for paperback. After talking with a few mentors, this pricing felt comfortable to me at the time, so I went with it.

Plus, I wanted to make sure I could use this pricing to my benefit for speaking gigs. When people booked me to speak and wanted to order books, I could give them a discount and charge $15 a book. Clients really appreciated that little gesture. All it took for me was to make the book $15.95, and I was able to do that. Had I priced the book at $12.95, I wouldn't have been able to offer the same discount, or if I did, I would have missed out on $3 for every book. When you speak to thousands of people, this adds up.

When I launched *The Elevated Entrepreneur*, I made the price $19.95 because we were using a free-plus-shipping funnel for the launch. A free-plus-shipping funnel is where I give someone the book for free and all they have to do is pay for the shipping. The shipping was $9.95, so by pricing my book at $19.95 on Amazon, it was a much better deal for someone to get the book from my funnel. This was huge for me because not only did I still get people buying my book, but I also collected their email address and information. On top of that, we upsold in the funnel, which allowed people to get familiar with and invest in some of my other products/services related to the book.

Overall Strategy

When you price your book, focus on your goals.

A great pricing strategy for many first-time authors is to launch your e-book at $0.99 to drive initial traffic and sales. Then, once you hit bestseller status or as your book builds momentum, start to raise your price weekly or monthly until you find a sweet spot. At that time, you can let your price settle.

For paperback, honestly, do what feels good to you. Think about your purpose and goals with the book. The higher the price, the more you earn per book. No matter what pricing you choose, always remember your intentions and your desire to help people.

Once your book is published, your book is officially live!

This does not mean your book is *launched*. Your publish date is the date your book goes live. Your launch date is when you send traffic to your book, and that is exactly what we are going to discuss next.

CHAPTER 16

Lucrative Launching

It was the middle of the pandemic, and someone came to me and asked if I helped with launching books. I immediately got geeked up and said yes. We jumped on a call so I could learn more about what she was looking for and how she would define a successful launch. I shared with her what I thought would be best based on her goals, and we struck a deal. A few weeks later, she launched her book and hit #1 bestseller in multiple categories including Mental Health & Eating Disorders.

She didn't hit the bestseller list by chance. She achieved this because she followed a system, and as you get ready to launch your book, you can use this exact system.

When it comes to launching your book, most people assume that you make it live, make a few social posts, and watch the sales roll in. Unfortunately, that is not the case.

If you want to have a successful, bestselling launch, it goes well beyond just making a few social posts.

I define a bestseller as a book that hits #1 in a particular category on Amazon. This is not top three in a category. It is not #1

New Release in a category. It is ranked #1 in a category. Unlike other lists where if you are top ten you are considered a bestseller, to be a bestseller on Amazon you need to be #1 in your category.

As we talk about launching your book and having a successful launch, I want you to think about why you wanted to write this book in the first place. Many of the authors we work with want to be a bestseller and use their book to ignite a podcast tour, obtain speaking gigs, generate leads, gain high-ticket clients, and more.

Your intention and reason for writing this book will play a big role in how you launch your book and which strategies you implement.

So let me ask you this . . .

Are you ready for your life to change?

Once you launch your book, you will find that opportunities arise that you never could have predicted. One of our clients launched her book, and within a week she signed a $4,000 client. Another one of our clients reached bestseller status in five categories. Another client was the #1 new release in seven categories. One of our clients was top 500 of all books on Amazon during his launch week. Another person we worked with got a huge speaking engagement at a major conference in their industry. Another client had her seven-year-old daughter tell her that it was her favorite book and she wants to write her own someday. I've been invited onto some of the top entrepreneurial podcasts because I launched a book that was relevant to their audience.

The list goes on and on and on, but in order to have great success with your book launch, your book needs to be as professional and legitimate as it can be. If you've followed the steps up to this point, you are ready to go.

If your book isn't professionally edited, it will hurt your launch.

If your cover sucks, no one will buy it.

If your formatting is amateurish, it will hurt your launch.

If your title is irrelevant and your subtitle is weak, it will hurt your launch.

If you hope and pray to hit bestseller status rather than doing the work, it will hurt your launch.

Launching a book into the world is an incredible honor and achievement. Celebrate the journey up to this point because you made it!

You have completed your book and are ready to change the world!

When I launched my first book, I had no email list, no audience, no following, and no clue what to do. I searched Google combing the internet to find any article I could on how to be a bestselling author.

I found thousands of results and I got to work. I tried anything and everything for my first book launch, and I mean everything. I did podcasts, paid IG shoutouts, a launch party, a launch team, speaking gigs, local meet-ups, grassroots marketing, texting everyone I knew, paid promotions, and more. I also spent hours and hours on the phone with CreateSpace (Amazon's self-publishing platform before it was called KDP).

When it came time to launch, I put everything into action, and on day one I hit my goal. I was a bestselling author. WOOHOO!

But I came across a major problem. I was exhausted. I was tired. And I had zero idea what worked and why I got to number one in multiple categories.

I knew there was a better way to launch, so two years later when I got ready to launch *Elevate Your Network*, I focused on working smarter not harder. I tried only a few of the strategies from the first time, and I did it again. I became a bestseller, and the results were better than before.

Fast-forward to the launch of *The Elevated Entrepreneur*, and I told myself that not only did I want the biggest launch yet, I wanted to do it with the least amount of stress. I reviewed my past launches, I created my game plan, I focused on the essentials, and on launch week, we had our biggest launch to date generating hundreds of leads and thousands of downloads.

I share this because after spending all this time on my own launches and countless hours researching and testing, I've found what works.

To have a bestselling launch, we need to focus on three main components: launch strategy, launch team, and quality reviews.

The Bestseller Launch Strategy

No matter what your ultimate goal of writing your book is, I always recommend shooting for a bestseller launch. If you're going to write a book, why not go big? Go big or go home! That's how I think.

Depending on your ultimate objective, you may decide to put more or less effort toward this, but either way I recommend you shoot for a bestseller launch.

Even though I talk about how book sales don't matter a crazy amount when growing your business, book sales are a key component to having your book become a bestseller during launch week.

As much as I want to help you, if your book doesn't get sales, it doesn't matter how great your strategy is. Visit www.bigideatobestseller.com/resources to get twenty-five marketing ideas to boost sales during launch week!

If no one knows who you are or what your book is about, it doesn't matter how great you are. No one will find your book or have their life changed. It's time for you to stop being the best kept secret and get your name and book into the hands of the people whose lives you can change!

The two launch strategies that you can use to hit the bestseller list are the free launch and the $0.99 launch.

When you run the free launch, you are in the free store on Kindle, meaning your book is competing against all the other free books. When you run the $0.99 launch, your book is on the paid Kindle store, meaning your book is competing against every single paid e-book on Amazon.

It is much easier to hit #1 on the free launch, which is why I recommend doing a three-day launch on the free store before switching to the $0.99 launch.

Plus, if you hit #1 on the free launch, you are a bestseller and can leverage that in your marketing to promote the $0.99 launch.

FREE Launch

The free launch is designed to get your book live and start driving awareness and early reviews.

The free launch is where you will have a small group of your closest people download the book and leave a review. This is also where we will run our first round of paid promotions (about $40) to drive massive downloads. This is not the time to share with everyone. That comes next. This is more of a behind-the-scenes launch to start building momentum and climbing the bestseller lists.

Step 1: Publish your book.

Step 2: Select your dates for a free promo (three days).

Step 3: Buy your paid promotions.

Step 4: Start your free launch and run paid promotions.

Step 5: Track downloads and take pictures of your bestseller ranking.

Step 6: Change your book to paid on day three of your free promo at noon PST.

When you do the free launch effectively, it jumpstarts your book and kicks off your launch.

Don't worry about losing money by giving your book away for free. Instead, focus on how many new people are going to get your book.

How many lives will be changed?

How many new leads can you bring in?

How many potential clients are you getting in front of?

Give it away for free now to make more later. By giving it away for free, you are giving yourself a better chance at #1, and being a bestseller pays way more over the lifespan of your book than getting a couple hundred bucks on the front end.

$0.99 Launch

The $0.99 launch is where we go all in! Let's gooooo!

This is when we have everyone we know including our loyal launch team buy the book, leave a review, and spread the word. It is officially launch day!

If you absolutely hate the idea of giving your book away for free, you don't have to. You can jump headfirst into the $0.99 launch.

I like to do the free launch behind the scenes leading up to the official launch day. If you want to launch your book on June 9, then I suggest you run the free launch June 6–8. Then on June 8, you switch it from free to paid, and on June 9, your launch begins.

Remember, your publish date is different from your launch date. Your publish date is the day the book goes live. Your launch date is the date you start driving people to your sales page and promote the book.

For the $0.99 strategy, it is a full send.

Here are some ideas to drive sales on launch day:

- Email your list and ask them to buy one or more copies.
- Post on your social media at least once per day.
- Text everyone in your phone book and ask them to buy your book.
- Ask your friends and family to support you.
- Invite your clients to buy your book.
- Do media interviews that have a direct link to your book as the call to action.

You can get creative with this. Your book will be $0.99 for about a week or until you change it, so have some fun with the launch.

For example, I wanted to try something different so I got on Instagram and said for the first ten people to buy the book, I'd do a fun giveaway with prizes. I made it a game and people loved it! That led to ten people sharing my book on social, which built awareness and proof.

When you do the $0.99 strategy, you will also want to use paid promotions to boost your sales. There are promo sites designed specifically for spreading the word about free or discounted e-books. Each promo site has thousands and thousands of avid readers searching for free and $0.99 books in your genre. They all have different levels of availability, so try booking these out weeks ahead of your official launch day.

As your book starts to climb the bestseller charts, make sure to screenshot your rankings. When I launched my first book, I refreshed the page every five minutes for the entire day because I was so excited. You don't have to check it every five minutes like I did because the rankings update every few hours. Just check it throughout the day and screenshot it as the rankings update.

Do NOT be shy during your launch week! You have worked your butt off to create a book that will change people's lives. Go all in on this launch and ask for support. Posting on social media is great, but combining it with reaching out to people directly is game-changing.

During my launches, I reach out to every person in my contact list and hundreds of my followers. I know social media is great, but it only shows my posts to some people. Reaching out directly definitely takes more time, but it is more personal and more likely to be seen.

If you want to have a great launch, don't be afraid to put in the work. As my man from the movie *We're the Millers* famously said, "No RAGRETS." Launch week only happens once, so make it happen!

If you follow this strategy, your book's bestseller ranking will skyrocket!

How To Build a Launch Team

A launch team is a group of people who want to support your book launch. Your launch team can be made up of anyone who wants to participate and support you.

Unlike with asking for certain advice, welcome whoever wants to support you on your book journey. It can be friends, family, colleagues, prospects, or clients. The number one goal is to get a bunch of people excited about your launch.

One thing that I found through my experience is when you launch a book, people come out of left field to support you. People you didn't even know follow you want to join. People you haven't spoken to since high school want to join. Writing a book is such a big accomplishment that people really want to help!

Building a launch team is a very clear-cut process. You offer things of value like your book for free, and they do things that help with your launch.

You give

- Advanced copy of the book (often a PDF)
- Access to bonuses
    - Q&A with you
    - Free course or one-on-one call

- Private Facebook group for launch team members only

You receive

- Social push
- Book purchase and download on launch week
- Introductions to podcast host, speaking gigs, local news stations, etc.

You cannot demand someone to give a review on your book, but you definitely want to encourage people on your launch team to leave an honest review.

By giving people access to the book early, they feel like they are part of your team. Depending on how early you create your launch team, you can include them in the acknowledgments as an added bonus.

When building your launch team, you want to make sure you have a way of communicating effectively with them. Depending on the size of your launch team, you may use a variety of platforms.

How To Get People on Your Launch Team

In order for your launch team to be successful, you must talk about your launch team. You must invite people and make it as easy as possible for them to join and participate.

Post on Social Media

One of the best ways to have people join your launch team

is to post on social media. When you post on social media, you can have them answer yes in a poll, visit a link to fill out an application, or send you a DM saying they're interested.

When you post on social media, this not only brings awareness to your upcoming launch, but it can draw people in. Make sure you talk about this more than once to give people the best chance of signing up.

Give a very clear window of your time frame for signing up. If you are filling up your launch team in a week, tell people time is limited. If you are filling up your launch team in three days, be super clear about that. People tend to wait until the last minute, so by posting frequently and clearly, you can ignite action.

Ask Directly

For a lot of first-time authors or people without a massive following, you may not get a crazy amount of responses from social media, and that is okay. If you don't get the response you want or even if you do, I recommend reaching out to people directly and asking them to be part of your launch team.

Before you feel weird asking people directly, please place your ego to the side and focus on the bigger picture of releasing your book and impacting a lot of people. This is your book! This is a big deal! Be proud and invite people to join you.

When you ask people directly, you get faster responses and more commitment, and people feel appreciated and wanted.

By thinking of them and inviting them to be on your launch team for your book, you've created a huge opportunity for connection!

No one will be as excited as you are because it's your book, but you definitely want to include people who are hyped, not just like, "Ehh, okay, I'll be on the team." Positive mojo is key!

Remember, our goal is to have people who want to help us promote the book and support the launch. If people say no or they don't want to participate, that is okay. They can buy the book once it's out. You want people who are excited to support you on your launch team!

Launch Team Application

If you choose to use an application, make sure to get the information you want. Just because someone applies to be on your launch team doesn't mean you have to accept them.

They can still support you even if they are not on the launch team. We want to make sure we build the right team, and in this case, it's people who are going to support you, bring the energy up, and have positive vibes.

Here's what to include on a launch team application:

- Name
- Email
- Social media handle(s)
- Are you willing to buy the book on Amazon? Yes/No

- Are you willing to leave an honest review after you purchase? Yes/No
- Are you willing to post on social media? Yes/No
- Do you have a podcast? And if so, would you be willing to have me as a guest? Yes/No
- Why are you interested in supporting the launch of [your book title]?
- What are some skills or characteristics you have that you want to contribute to this launch?
- Are there any people you can connect me with to boost awareness of the book (podcast hosts, media outlets, etc.)? If so, please list their names and a little background on them.

Every question serves a purpose that will help you see how much the applicant wants to help and support you. A bare minimum is that they say they'll buy the book, leave a review, and post on social. You can choose to include more questions if you desire, but the key is to ask questions that help you get the information you want.

This gets fun when someone says they know someone on TV who would love to interview you or when they know someone who runs a company who wants to buy one hundred copies for their team or staff.

BOOM! Magic is happening already.

How To Communicate with Your Launch Team

Once you have your launch team, communication is the name of the game! You need to be super clear and straightforward in your asks. When someone signs up to be on your launch team, make it clear what to expect and when to execute.

This isn't some roundabout sales pitch. This is you launching your book, and anyone who joins your launch team is here to support you.

You have a lot to do when it comes time to launch your book, and you will be incredibly excited! Make sure that you communicate openly and honestly with your launch team. The clearer you are, the easier it becomes for people to support you.

To communicate with your launch team, you can use

- Email blasts with members only
- Facebook group
- Slack channel
- Telegram group

I tend to recommend email blasts and groups with a combination of texts and personalization throughout the process.

Figure out what works best for you and for your launch team members. If they don't see your emails or posts, they won't know what to do. The key here is to create a method of communication that makes it easy for everyone to engage, communicate, and participate.

Launch teams can vary greatly in size. For many new authors, you might have ten to thirty people on your launch team. For authors with a huge following, you might have one or two hundred people.

Don't worry too much about the size. Instead, focus on making sure everyone on board is as active and engaged as possible because no matter how big your launch team is, there will always be people who do more than asked and people who don't do anything at all.

Yes, even if people sign up, they still might forget to do one of the tasks you're looking for. That is why it is so important to be clear and concise with your asks. Last, always follow up with your launch team members. People are busy and sometimes they need to be reminded.

How To Get Reviews

When it comes time to launch your book, book reviews are incredibly valuable. Not only does it create massive social proof, but it signals to Amazon that people are liking your book and that they should show it to more potential readers.

I don't know about you, but a book with fifty-plus reviews is much easier for me to buy than a book with zero reviews.

There are two types of reviews: verified and unverified.

- Verified reviews are from people who have downloaded your book or purchased your book.
- Unverified reviews are people who leave a review but haven't gotten the book from Amazon.

When you launch your book, you want as many reviews as possible to be verified because they are much more effective. This is why it is so important for your launch team to purchase the book before leaving a review. Super important note: You cannot pay someone for a review as that is against the rules. However, you can encourage people to leave an honest review once they've gotten the book.

Here's how to get book reviews for your book:

Ask Your Launch Team for Reviews

If you set up your launch team effectively, this should be an easy ask. We've already encouraged people to leave a review; we just need to guide them on what to do.

Focus on making this as clear as you possibly can. The less friction someone has, the more likely they are to actually leave you the review. Even though people have decided they want to leave a review, don't be shocked if you have to remind them a few times.

You aren't being annoying. You are being persistent. This is your freaking book launch for crying out loud!

Ask Your Contacts

When you release your book, it's time to go all in on marketing. Reach out to people you know and invite them to read your book and leave an honest review. You might be surprised at how many people will want to support you.

Ask Your Readers

In your book, you can literally have a page in the book that asks people to leave a review if they liked your book. Just include the link and an image of your book and let them do the rest.

In this book, I invited you to leave a review earlier. I put my ask in the middle rather than the end of the book because I know a lot of people don't finish books, and I wanted to make the ask earlier. Where you put your review ask is entirely up to you.

Ask People who Tell You They Read Your Book

Once your book is out, people are going to tell you their favorite parts, how it changed their life, and so much more. When people reach out to tell you this, say thank you, continue the conversation, and ask if they would be interested in leaving you a review so more people can have the chance to have their life changed.

Special Review Link

Here's what most authors do. They ask someone to leave them a review and send them to the book sales page. From there, they hope the potential reviewer will scroll down and search for the spot that says write/leave a review.

While this can be effective if the person hasn't read the book yet, this can make it much more difficult for someone to actually leave a review.

If you know they've already downloaded or purchased your book, you can actually send them directly to a review page.

This can make a huge difference because it makes it so much easier for the reader to leave a review.

Here is the review link to use: Amazon.com/review/create-review?&asin=ADDYOURINFOHERE

Step 1: Visit your book sales page.

Step 2: Copy the ISBN or ASIN.

Step 3: Add the ISBN or ASIN to the link above.

Step 4: Create a short link (bit.ly link) that's easy to remember and share.

Step 5: Share new link with your people to leave a review.

Here is an example for my book *The Elevated Entrepreneur*.

- Book sales page: https://www.amazon.com/Elevated-Entrepreneur-Unlocking-Performers-Entrepreneurs-ebook/dp/B09J2WDJYZ
- ISBN: B09J2WDJYZ
- Review page: Amazon.com/review/create-review?&asin=B09J2WDJYZ

When you combine a strong launch strategy with a dedicated launch team and quality reviews, you set yourself up to have an incredible and unforgettable launch!

CHAPTER 17

After the Launch

You've launched your book and are asking yourself, "NOW WHAT?"

While the goal of this book is to get you to this point and teach you everything you need to know to write, publish, and launch a nonfiction book, I don't want you to stop here. I want you to take your book and turn it into the business empire of your dreams.

When you have a book, you can build a business on the back end or you can take your existing business to the next level.

I've helped people who are just starting out write their book, and I've helped people with seven- or eight-figure companies write their book.

If you are just starting out, your book can help you create clarity, be used as the framework for your coaching offer, or kickstart your business.

If you already have a successful business, you can use your book to raise your speaking/coaching fees, get top national media, or increase your lead flow at volume.

Wherever you are in your business, a book provides you with the chance to create more for yourself.

Hard truth: If you don't market your book, no one will. You are the ultimate salesperson for your book. Whether you hate sales or love sales, you are the best salesperson for your book. No one knows it better than you. No one will be as excited about it as you. Use this! Once you launch, don't stop talking about it. Talk about it even more. Share reviews. Share results people are getting after reading it.

11 Ways To Make Money from Your Book

Making money is awesome. Making an impact on a global scale is incredible. Doing both at the same time is the *best*.

A book is more than just a book. A book is your vehicle to growing your business.

Not only can a book bring you leads, get you booked on top media, and grow your audience, but it can generate tons of revenue.

One of my good friends wrote her first book after attending a personal development conference, and it changed her life. She went from never having written a book to having five bestselling and award-winning books, a Guinness World Record, a TEDx talk, speaking opportunities and an impact on thousands of people, and hundreds of thousands of dollars in profit in her business.

A book opens the door for incredible opportunity!

Most marketing strategies help you with one result at a time. Few marketing strategies do as much as a book. A book provides you with a ton of options at every stage of your business journey. The most amazing part of having a book is when you know what you are doing, you can generate revenue before the book is even released.

To get you started with how to leverage your book for business growth, here are eleven ways to make money from your book. You can try one or all, but the key is to figure out what fits best with your vision, business, and skill set.

#1 –Coaching Clients

One of the most popular ways for entrepreneurs, thought leaders, and experts to monetize their book is through a back-end offer of coaching. This can be done in a one-on-one or group setting.

Oftentimes, writing a book will help you expand your authority to the point that people start hiring you on your book topic.

#2 –Speaking Gigs

Speaking engagements are a fantastic way to make money from your book because your book can serve as a marketing tool before speaking engagements (to book them) and after (to get paid from the people you spoke to).

As a speaker, you can charge a fee and get paid up front for your services. One of my favorite strategies to land paid speaking engagements is to attend events or find people online who hire speakers for conferences. Then I send them copies of my book and start to build a relationship. Once the relationships grow and develop, you'll start to get hired. Using your book as the entry point to paid gigs is incredible because it is a great way to get your name out there and break the ice with someone you've never met without immediately pitching them.

Once you are hired, you can often sell copies in the back of the room. This can easily increase your revenue. I spoke to a group of 150 high schoolers at a summer conference. After, I sold my book for $15 and sold fifty copies. That was a quick $450 in thirty minutes. Plus, fifty new people had my book and the vehicle to change their life.

The last thing to mention here is when you have a book, you can increase your speaking fees right away. If you have a book but are priced too low, it can actually harm you. People will be confused why your prices are too low. Instead, use your book to raise your fees and command a higher price. You are the expert!

#3 –Online Course/Digital Products

When you have a book, you have the framework for an entire course. You can literally take your book and create a course based on the content. Add some additional value-based deliverables, video content, support, and boom, you have a course that you can sell.

You can also use your book to create digital products like masterclasses, templates, and more. The easiest way to do this is to take a chapter or a main concept and elaborate on it in a way that will help the reader go deeper on that particular topic.

#4 –Masterminds/Retreats

Masterminds are a group of people who come together to achieve their goals. They are often led by one person who brings the group together and are filled with like-minded people who desire some form of next-level result. The right mastermind can massively level up your life and your business. Masterminds are also really great to funnel your book readers into.

If you like to bring people together under one roof to create epic experiences and transformations, you can use your book to fill spots in your mastermind or your retreats.

When people read your book, they get to know and trust you. Those are huge factors when it comes to making investment decisions.

#5 –Physical Products

If you have an e-commerce company that sells physical products, a book will be huge.

A book is your ticket to build a relationship with your reader. When people know you and understand the way you think, they are more likely to feel connected to you. That connection is incredibly powerful when it comes to making purchasing decisions and trying out your product.

By having a book, you build a connection that directly translates to the sales of your product. People want to feel more connected to the brands they buy from, and by sharing the journey, you open up huge doors.

It's bigger than a book!

Dave Asprey, the bestselling author of *The Bulletproof Diet*, has sold a lot of coffee due to writing his book. I know I've bought products or supported major brands after reading their founder's book.

#6 –Live Events

If you've ever wanted to host your own live events, having a book might be the answer you've been looking for.

When you have a book, you invite people to learn about who you are and what you do. When you have a great book, it inspires people to take action and follow your journey.

As you build your following, you can create live events and workshops based on the topics of your book and invite your readers to join you. This is a wonderful way to sell tickets and bring people together.

#7 –Investing Opportunities

Writing a great book can bring you investing opportunities. If you are in real estate and write a great book, people will start to reach out to you more. One of our clients is an incredible real estate investor, and by writing his book, he opened the door for deals to be brought to him.

Since he wrote the book on it, people trust that he can help them with their problem. The book gave them a peek behind the curtain of what partnering with him could lead to. This has led to him having more customers, but this has also led to him getting more opportunities to invest with his readers.

When people know who you are and what you do, it becomes easier for them to know how to work with you. We all want to win and by having a book, you create a clear pathway.

#8 –Agency Clients/Done-for-You Services

Writing a great book establishes you as the expert on what you do. If you run a social media agency and have a book that showcases your process and your results, people will want to work with you.

If you offer a done-for-you service and your book shows people what you do and how it will make their life easier, people will want to hire you.

If you have a process and you teach that in your book, people will start to see how it can work for them, and naturally, they'll want to try it out and get the results you and your clients have gotten.

#9 –Career Transition

One of our clients came to me wanting to use a book to jumpstart a new career. She's had great success in the corporate world but wanted to do something else. She wrote a book based on the skills she had in order to help more women create career opportunities and improve their leadership. By doing this, she boosted her credibility by becoming an author and was more easily able to switch careers.

Not only can this increase your happiness, but it can help you change industries more easily and leverage a pay raise.

#10 –Networking Opportunities (Affiliates & Referral Partners)

Affiliates and referral partners are incredible opportunities when you have a book. I've had people read my book and then ask how they can promote me and my programs. They've never met me, but because they read my book, they want to promote me.

Depending on the type of affiliate program you offer, people can make thousands of dollars selling your programs. For example, let's say you have a $5,000 product. If someone reads your book and loves what you do, they can become an affiliate and sell your program. If they get 20% per sale, that's $1,000. If they sell five programs, that's an extra $5,000 for them and $20,000 for you. Talk about a win-win opportunity!

If you get ten readers to become advocates for your brand, you and they can both make a lot of money through affiliate deals and referral agreements.

#11 –Book Sales

I mentioned this earlier, but I'll say it again. For most authors, book sales are a bonus. I want you to sell a shit-ton of books, and when you do, all of that money will be a wonderful surprise come the end of the month.

I have a friend who leveraged his book as a first-time author to sell ten thousand–plus copies in a year. That led to him making some great money and securing a traditional publishing deal.

Another one of our clients did such a great job promoting her book that during launch week, a publishing company came to her asking if she'd write a second book with them. She said yes and received a huge advance.

It's bigger than a book! Write a book one time, and you can use it to create more opportunities than you ever thought possible.

BONUS CHAPTER

How To Turn Your Book into 100+ Pieces of Content

We've talked about writing a book. We've talked about how to make it a bestseller. Now, in this bonus chapter, I'm going to show you how to turn your book into over one hundred pieces of social content and save hundreds of hours in the process.

When most people write a book, they just write a book. When you and I write a book, not only do we create something of incredible value but we use it to create additional content and opportunities.

We put in the work once and then leverage it over and over again to save us time.

Instead of just writing a book, we can use the book as an outline for social media content, enhanced course creation, or even to develop a coaching program.

When it comes to content creation, a lot of people spend hours and hours first trying to come up with content and then even more time trying to actually create the content.

By writing a book with the process we've discussed in this book, your book will be optimized to leverage for content ideas and creation.

If you have a team behind you, share your outline and book and let them create from there. If you are solo, you can plug and play.

When I tell people that their book is an incredible vehicle for social content, they get worried that they are giving too much away or people will see too much. The exact opposite is true. People need to hear things more than once (especially good quality content), *and* people love to consume similar information in different ways. The more value you give for free, the more they're going to want to see what is behind the paywall.

For example, when I wrote *The Elevated Entrepreneur*, I turned the book into a ton of content pieces.

- Hundreds of stories from idea to launch
- 3 IG reels series totaling 15 videos
- Live videos teaching what I learned
- A live IG show interviewing people
- Carousels sharing best practices and tips

The list goes on and on. By writing my book, I had all my ideas on paper, which made it easy to turn them into content pieces. I took content that I had already created for the book and repurposed it for social media. These content pieces doubled as high-quality content and book promotion ultimately leading to more sales, more reviews, and more connection with my audience.

The Two Angles for Your Book Content

The really cool thing when it comes to creating content with your book is you have multiple angles that add value to the reader.

#1 — Education-Based Content for the Reader

This is where you add value by educating your audience. You can share stories, testimonials, top tips, recommendations, etc., from your book that immediately teaches your reader something. This is all about helping solve problems and getting results.

Your goal is to teach the content you share in your book on social.

#2 – Journey-Based Content from the Author's Experience

This is where you document the process. Your audience will feel they are a part of your book journey and be more likely to get invested in your success. The key with this is to document yourself as you experience the process of writing a book. It can be really effective to create a story highlight on Instagram with a title like "BOOK PROCESS" or "FIRST BOOK."

Your goal is to document your book journey and share what you do as you do it. People love to see people walk the walk and go through the journey rather than just talk about the results.

Between these two types of content, you've created insane value, and you've made yourself someone that your audience can really connect with and come with on the journey.

Content Types

Before I share with you a ton of ways to create more than one hundred pieces of content, let's go over some different types of content you can create from your book.

- Story Posts
    - Polls
    - Quizzes
    - Questions
    - Countdowns
- Carousel Graphics
    - Top tips
    - Big lessons
    - Small paragraphs broken into single-sentence slides
- Live Video
    - Short, 1–3 min
    - Long, 4–12 min
- Reels
    - Education
    - Story based
    - Series
    - Trending sounds
- Static Images
    - Quotes
    - Images of you with a caption/story
- Long-Form Copy/Captions

A lot of the content ideas I share can be made for one platform and then repurposed for multiple platforms.

Milestone Content Ideas

Writing a book is an incredible accomplishment. Sharing when you hit milestones are great for social as it updates your audience, shows your progress, holds you accountable, and celebrates your wins!

You can share these in a variety of ways, but I typically recommend you do this via stories and then maybe make a compilation video/carousel for your feed to highlight the process. Here are some milestones you can share.

- Announce your decision to write a book.
- Poll the audience about their interest in your topic (potential clients).
- First words on the page.
- Finished first chapter/writing session.
- Finished first draft—a huge accomplishment.
- Sending your book to an editor.
- Share your sample cover designs.
- Share the cover you selected.
- Announce launch date.
- Received the first printed copy.
- The week leading up to launch.
- Launch day.
- Launch week.
- Highlight any PR events (podcasts, writeups, people sharing on social).
- Screenshots of the launch and rankings.

Poll Ideas

One of the most effective ways to create engagement is to poll the audience. The questions can be simple. Your goal here is to get engagement, not necessarily have groundbreaking, ultra-creative, first-of-its-kind content.

Here are a couple of ideas to get you started:

- Which cover do you like best?
- Are you more interested in X or Y?
- Do you want behind the scenes of writing a book?
- Are you excited about [topic]?
- Would you be interested in this resource if I included it in the book?

If you want people to give their opinion or offer their own suggestions, feel free to ask an open-ended question instead.

Chapter-by-Chapter Content

- Your favorite/best quote from the chapter.
- Create a video sharing a story that you used.
- Share a testimonial you used in the chapter.
- Create a three-tips or five-secrets reel based on the content in the chapter.
- Design a carousel for your main talking point/lesson in the chapter.

If you have ten chapters, this can easily be fifty-plus pieces of content right off the bat. Then take this content and share it on your other platforms for maximum reach and exposure.

The Process Content

- Weekly progress –Provide an update on what you did (good and bad).
- Monthly progress –Where are you in the process?
- How much do you have left in the process?
- What comes next in the process? (People want to see you actually doing it.)
- Crossing off book to-do list as you complete each phase.

Launch Content

- When the book is set to launch
- When you hold the book for the first time
- When you get a bunch of copies in the mail
- When the book is up on Amazon
- Launch day announcement
- Early reviews
- Screenshots of rankings
- Pictures of people with the book
- Reshares of podcasts you are featured in
- Reshares from people posting about your book

When you execute on these ideas, you will easily have over one hundred pieces of content from the time you decide to write a book until the time you are deep into your launch. If you commit to executing, you will have clients ready to buy, a deeper connection with your audience, and saved time from trying to come up with new ideas.

Get a free social media checklist at www.bigideatobestseller.com/resources.

The Exact Roadmap from Big Idea To Bestseller

Congratulations! You made it.

You now know what it takes to turn your big idea into a bestseller.

If you were to tell me the day I signed my contract to work for the Los Angeles Lakers that I would have a rapidly growing business helping people write and launch nonfiction books, I would've thought you were crazy.

I thought my future was planned out: Be a sports agent. Make millions of dollars. Represent the greatest NBA athletes in the world. Buy a house. Buy an island. Get married. Have kids.

Then once I did all of that, I would write books, speak on stages, and give back.

But life doesn't always go according to plan.

Instead, I retired from the Lakers with Kobe and launched my first bestseller at twenty-three.

And that is the beauty of the game of life. We may not always control what happens to us, but we always control how we respond. We all have a story to tell. We've all been thrown into situations we never could have expected. And now, here you are, reading this book.

Our journeys have led us to this very moment, and we're stronger because of it.

You're reading this book because you want more. You've had an itch or a calling to write your book. Everything you've done has led to you reading this very word.

You can read this book and do nothing.

Or . . .

You can read this book and change your life.

This book is the roadmap.

All you need to do is follow the steps below and the content in this book to turn your dream of writing a book into your reality!

Here is the roadmap to your first bestselling book:

1. Get started with a great idea.
2. Map out an organized outline.
3. Write a doggy draft.
4. Do some selective self-editing.
5. Hire elite editors.
6. Choose a title and subtitle that sells.
7. Create a cover that converts with a professional cover designer.

8. Focus on formatting with a professional book formatter.
9. Professionally publish your book on KDP.
10. Launch your book!

When you follow this roadmap, you can turn your big idea into a bestselling book in less than six months.

You have the skills.

You have the knowledge.

You have the experience.

It's time to write your book!

Here's What To Do Next

It's bigger than a book!

Whenever you're ready, here are four ways we can help you take the next step on your book journey:

1. Access All Your Free Bonuses

By reading this book and saying yes to yourself, you have unlocked every bonus and resource in this book.

Visit www.bigideatobestseller.com/resources to get all the resources mentioned in this book for free.

2. Join Big Idea To Bestseller and Write Your Book

If you found this book helpful and want some help writing and launching your first or next book, I'd love to invite you to chat with me and our team.

Visit www.bigideatobestseller.com/call to schedule a call with our team to discuss your book game plan.

3. Hire Jake To Speak

If you are looking for a high-energy hype man of a motivational speaker for your conference, event, or mastermind, I'd love to bring it!

Email jake@jakekelfer.com with "SPEAKING" in the subject line.

4. Connect on Social Media

Let's keep the convo going! The journey doesn't end here. I'd love to connect with you on all social platforms. Let's have some fun!

You can find me on social at @jakekelfer.

Acknowledgments

This book would not be in your hands right now if it weren't for some amazing people, so it's time for some shoutouts!

BIG SHOUTOUT: I'd like to thank my parents, Dave and Sheri, and my brother, Jonah for your endless support. Knowing that I always have you guys in my corner means the world to me.

BIG SHOUTOUT: I'd like to thank my girlfriend, Jenna, for listening to me for hours and hours about this book and how it's going to impact the world. Thank you for supporting me, encouraging me, and being there for me. Thank you for tolerating my super early alarms and checking in with me every step of the way.

BIG SHOUTOUT: I'd like to thank my assistant, Meredith, for absolutely crushing it! Thank you for giving me the space to create and keeping me accountable. I appreciate your attention to detail and excitement throughout this entire process!

BIG SHOUTOUT: I'd like to thank my team for putting this book together and making it so legit! Shoutout to my editor, Carly Catt, design team at 100Covers, and my formatter.

BIG SHOUTOUT: I'd like to thank my coach, Chris Harder, for inspiring me and challenging me to write this book and do the Project Bestseller challenge. He pushed me and believed in me, and I'm so grateful he did.

BIG SHOUTOUT: A big thank-you goes to Jess DeRose who inspired me to make Big Idea To Bestseller the program it is today.

BIG SHOUTOUT: Thank you to everyone who participated in Project Bestseller. I wrote this book in real time, with daily updates sharing my progress every step of the way. I'm so blessed that you participated in this challenge, and I'm so grateful for all of your support, encouragement, and questions.

BIG SHOUTOUT: Thank you to all of my friends and clients in the Big Idea To Bestseller program. You are all superstars in your own way, and I'm so grateful to be your coach. Keep changing the world with your books!

BIG SHOUTOUT: A big thank-you to YOU. Thank you for choosing to invest your time, money, and energy into reading this book. I can't wait to see your book hit bestseller status!

About the Author

Jake Kelfer is a lifestyle entrepreneur, life elevator, and coach to ambitious entrepreneurs and freedom seekers helping people write and launch bestselling books. He is the creator of Big Idea To Bestseller which helps coaches and entrepreneurs write, publish, and launch nonfiction books to grow their businesses and make an impact. He is a 3x bestselling author, a high-energy motivational speaker and hype man, investor, and the founder of the Professional Basketball Combine, which helped 70+ NBA draft prospects turn their dreams of playing pro basketball into their reality. He and his work have been featured on *Forbes, Sports Illustrated, ESPN,* and many other major media outlets. Connect with Jake on social at @jakekelfer!

Made in the USA
Columbia, SC
24 February 2023